AND, MAN MADE GOD IN HIS OWN IMAGE

THE MISBEGOTTEN MORMON DOCTRINE OF DEITY

Bill Grover

NEW HARBOR PRESS

RAPID CITY, SD

Grover/New Harbor Press

1601 Mt. Rushmore Rd Ste 3288

Rapid City, SD 57701

www.NewHarborPress.com

Ordering Information:

Quantity sales. Special discounts are available on quantity purchases by corporations, associations, and others. For details, contact the "Special Sales Department" at the address above.

And, Man Made God in His Own Image/Bill Grover. -- 1st ed.

ISBN 978-1-63357-408-3

CONTENTS

INTRODUCTION

Ten Reasons

A Mormon lady, whom I'm sure is a good and kind person, has compiled a list of ten reasons telling us why we all should become Mormons.[1]

(1). She says "Jesus Christ is the center of the Mormon faith."

But He is also the center of the faith of Roman Catholics and the evangelical Protestant denominations. The issue should not be whether the word "Christ" is part of a religion's name or is prominent in a religion's literature but whether one's doctrines faithfully teach the Jesus of the Bible. Calling their faith "The Church of Jesus Christ" is not proof that it teaches the truth about Jesus. Note, for example, that the Mormon religion states that Christ was a "spirit child" in heaven.[2] But where does the Bible say that? This illustrates that Mormons teach doctrines about our Lord Jesus which are not found in the Bible. Yes, a "Christ" may be the center of the Mormon religion, but the question is, "is that the same Christ of the Scriptures?"

(2). She says "God still speaks to the world through a prophet."

But even if there are modern prophets, New Testament prophets very clearly did not control the Christian church's doctrine as Joe Smith does for Mormons. Instead, they predicted natural events as a famine (Acts 11:28) or Paul's arrest (Acts 21:10) or exhorted believers (Acts 15:32). The notion that a modern prophet named Smith should arise to supremely dictate tenets which the church must abide by scrapes against the apostolic requirement that prophets are to subordinate themselves to the teachings of Paul. (1 Corinthians 14:37) That is, to the Bible! It was the original apostles who were promised inerrancy (John 16:13) not a 19th century "prophet."

(3). She says "The Book of Mormon is more evidence of Christ."

But more evidence of what in particular about Christ? In reviewing the teachings about Jesus in books as 1 & 2 Nephi, Jacob, Mosiah, and Ether, theologically speaking, I do not see helpful additions to our knowledge of the Person of our Lord over what the Bible, itself, teaches. Are we to believe that it was God's will to hide important information from faithful believers for centuries which was only to be later discovered by Joe Smith? I think not!

(4). She says, "We have no paid clergy."

But why is this thought to be biblical? Has she not read the apostle's teaching in 1 Timothy5:17, 18?

> Let the elders who rule well be counted worthy of double honor, especially those who labor in the word and doctrine. For the Scripture says 'You shall not muzzle an ox while it treads out the grain, and 'the laborer is worthy of his wages.

(5). She says, "We have the biggest missionary program."

And, I can believe that. Just today in my neighborhood I saw two young Mormon missionaries going door to door. But I once asked another of these, "Have you read Joseph Smith's translation of the Bible? What textual evidence in your view-- like ancient copies of the Bible and so forth--supports Smith's addition of many verses to the King James Version and his omission of others?" It was clear that the Mormon missionaries had no idea of what I was talking about; they had neither read Joe's translation nor could they defend their prophet on this matter even if they had been aware of "The Inspired Version." And, I think that the persons in my neighborhood to whom Mormons witness know even less about the Smith's teachings. Ignorance is an opening. So, if you are a Mormon reading this, can you justify Joe's additions and omissions to the Bible in his "Inspired Version" like Genesis 50: 30,33 and his removing Mark 13:32 from his translation? If you cannot, should this not cause you to question your belief in Smith's capabilities?

(6). She says, "We know death does not separate families."

I take this as a reference to the Mormon doctrine of celestial marriage wherein the family unit continues if the married individuals keep all the terms and conditions of the Mormon priesthood; they become married for eternity.[3] However, that this is not a teaching found in the Bible is evident by Scriptures as Romans 7:2 where if the spouse of a married person dies, the other is free to remarry. Paul does not qualify by adding, "Of course, **if** they are married for eternity, she must not remarry." Note that the inspired apostle nowhere in his writings says anything about the possibility of marriage for eternity, and it is not a tenet affirmed in any other biblical text either. It is purely a Mormon invention. But one will realize the lure of eternal marriage for those thinking about becoming Mormons. Mormons use the love of one's spouse to get converts.

(7). She says, "We have temples."

Okay, but where in the New Testament are there Christian temples as places of worship or places where Christian rites are performed? There are no such Christian temples in the Bible. These temples too are Mormon inventions. But what advantages are temples to Mormons? Why, only in Mormon temples can marriage for eternity or even water baptism take place.[4] Just imagine, you can only be baptized in a temple. But where is that taught in the Bible? It is not. In the New Testament baptism occurred on places like the road to Gaza (Acts 8:38) or a house (Acts 10:48); it is not said that it occurred in "temples." So, where is the biblical justification to limit it to taking place in Mormon temples?

(8). She says, "We have authority from God through a prophet."

But as noted above, in the Bible the prophet is not given authority over the church. That status does belong to Paul (1 Corinthians 14:37), and, of course, to other New Testament apostles. And, so it is the teachings of Paul which are to be understood and followed, "Hold fast the pattern of sound words which you have heard from me." (2 Timothy 1:13). In contrast,

AND, MAN MADE GOD IN HIS OWN IMAGE

the words of prophets are instead open to critical evaluation. "Let two or three prophets speak, and let the others judge." (1 Corinthians 14:29). The sayings of prophets should be judged according to Paul. But while I have read the writings of many Mormons, I have yet to see in them any examples of Joseph Smith's teachings being judged. This is another example of Mormons not following the Bible. Instead, read the words of a Mormon hymn to the most wonderful Joe:

> Praise to the man who communed with Jehovah,
> Jesus anointed that prophet and seer,
> Blessed to open the last dispensation,
> Kings shall extoll him and nations revere.
> Hail to the Prophet ascended to heaven,
> Traitors and tyrants now fight him in vain
> Mingling with Gods, he can plan for his brethren,
> Death cannot conquer the hero again. (Gospel Principles, 358, 359).

(9). She says, "We are not perfect but we have the same goals."

And, that is a nice confession. But it is hopeful that not many Mormons have the same goal as did their prophet. Their lustful prophet Joe speaks through God who commands and threatens Joe's wife, Emma, to let Joe have more wives (Doctrines and Covenants 132:52-56.) This despite the Bible's command that church leaders are to have only one wife (1 Timothy 3:2)! And recall our Savior's reference to only one woman for one man in marriage (Matthew 19:5). Note again 1 Corinthians 6:10:

only one wife! But does any Mormon ever criticize prophet Joe for his lust? Not that I can see. If you are a Mormon, explain why you think it is OK for Joe to ignore 1 Timothy 3:2.

(10.) She says, "We can have happiness forever."

Well, let's qualify that. In my view living eternally outside of God's presence is not a formula for happiness. But acquiring eternal life in Mormonism-- living in God's presence forever (unlike simple immortality which, even for unbelievers, is free[5])--requires obedience. And whom must Mormons obey? Plainly, it is the living prophet whose teachings must be followed completely[6] in Mormonism not the teachings of the Bible. So, if Joe the great and inerrant prophet, demands that Emma receive Joe's new brides, we just must accept that. Ummm yep! God said it! Joe said God said it! And, Joe is never, ever wrong! And, if I don't believe Joe, have I not lost my chance for exaltation? In my view such choices as that are not conducive to happiness.

Criterion for Determining Theological Mistakes

Every response I've made to the ten reasons advanced by this good Mormon woman contains an allusion to the Bible. Why? It is because the Bible is to be the standard by which we judge religious teaching:

All Scripture is given by inspiration of God and is profitable for doctrine, for reproof, for correction, for instruction in righteousness, that the man of God might be complete, thoroughly equipped for every good work. (2 Timothy 3:16, 17 my emphasis)

And, one needs to remember that Paul added his teachings to that standard in 2 Timothy 1:13, ("Hold fast the pattern of sound words which you have heard from me"), and that the other apostles in John 16:13 would be guided into "all truth" as well. But nowhere in the Bible does it ever foretell the inspiration and authority of Joseph Smith except of course in Joe's incredibly vain and silly additions to Genesis 50 in his "inspired" translation.[7] Joe wrote himself into the Bible! Has there ever been such conceit by any man? And, so when I entitle this book "Mistakes in the Mormon Doctrine of Deity" I will be evaluating Mormon teaching by the Bible, that is, by the real Bible not Joe's.

Importance of the Doctrine of God

I have already expressed my disagreement with several Mormon doctrines, and below I will explain more why I disagree with their teaching about the Bible. But the doctrine of God must be considered paramount to anyone who holds faith in a supreme Being. Belief in the nature of the one God which includes the divinity of Jesus Christ is what distinguishes Christianity from other religions. So, for example, Baptists immerse but Presbyterians think effusion is fine. Yet, both have very similar views about God. Calvinists believe in limitations on man's will to choose God. But Arminians teach prevenient grace. Yet, both affirm that the three Persons in God exist as one Being in one undivided essence. Pentecostals speak in tongues. But most other Protestants do not. Yet both believe the Father, Son, and Holy Spirit comprise one God. It is the doctrine of God, therefore, which unites evangelicals. Mormons, however, have veered off from that belief, and that is why I write.

Reorganized Church

I should qualify that the subject of this book is the Latter-Day Saints who under Brigham Young became established in Utah. I do not refer to the "Reorganized Church" with headquarters in Missouri. The latter, while claiming to follow the teachings of Joseph Smith refute some major doctrinal positions held by the LDS regarding God. First, the Reorganized Church denies the plurality of God; it teaches that there is only one God not three or many. Second, unlike the Utah branch which says that God changes as He once was a man, the Reorganized Church denies the mutability of God. Third, while Brigham Young can be understood as teaching that Adam is our God, the Missouri church disputes that as being heresy. These sentiments can be found in Ralston's work *"Fundamental Differences."*[8]

Status of Joseph Smith and Mormon Presidents

In my opinion the handicapping disadvantage of Mormon writers in biblical interpretation is that they are constrained to make their hermeneutics concur fully with the teachings of the supposedly inerrant teachings of Joe Smith and, later Mormon prophets and church presidents. The pedestals these "prophets" are placed upon in LDS doctrine reeks of disconformity to biblical principles. As said above, the Bible knows nothing about New Testament prophets dictating doctrines or rules to the church, and the lists of church special callings or offices as in Ephesians 4:7-12 make no mention of "church presidents."

Yet, despite the inability to garner any support for their supposedly inspired prophets and presidents from the Bible, the LDS endow these church leaders with an authority never to be questioned. This is evident, for example, in the following remarkable and wholly unbiblical direct quotation:

> We have a prophet living on earth today. This prophet is the president of The Church of Jesus Christ of latter- Day Saints. He has the right to revelation for the entire Church. He holds the "keys of the kingdom" meaning that he has the right to control the administration of the ordinances (see Matthew 16:19). No person except the chosen prophet and president can receive God's will for the membership of the Church. We should do those things the prophets tell us to do.[9]

So, what is the rationale for clothing Joe with such authority? The bold, unmitigated evidence is in The Doctrines and Covenants which Elder-Apostle John Taylor, authored: "Joseph Smith, the Prophet and Seer of the Lord, has done more, save Jesus only, for the salvation of men in this world than any other man that lived in it."[10] What, more than Moses? Oh yeah! What, more than Paul? Oh yeah! What, more than the apostle John? Oh yeah! Joe is supreme even over the authors of the Bible.

Therefore, I have no conviction that my logic herein will motivate a devoted Mormon to question his or her faith by my exposition of the Bible. Mormons believe that Joe Smith is greater than even the authors of Scripture. The Mormons and I simply have a different standard for determining truth.

Mormon Lip Service to the Bible

But I am not saying that Mormons entirely disregard the Bible. The King James Version is considered one of the four Mormon scriptures along with the book of Mormon, Doctrines and Covenants, and the Pearl of Great Price. However, the Bible is not regarded as inerrant. Instead, the wording and content of the Bible is considered unreliable. This is evident in Joe's adding and eliminating whole verses from the text and changing wording within verses. For example, Joe added verses 30, 33 to Genesis 50 in an attempt to authenticate his coming as the prophet. Also, Joe removed 13:32 from Mark likely due to his errant belief that Christ has only one nature which has all knowledge . Further, Joe changes words in verses to force the Bible to conform to his theology as in his translation of John 4:24. "God is Spirit" becomes "God promised His Spirit"! One can view these changes to the Bible in Joe's "Inspired Version."[11] In all, Joe made 3,410 changes to the Scriptures![12] Clearly, in Mormonism, Joseph Smith's opinions are more to be trusted than the Bible itself.

By the way, there is no textual justification for Joe's changing the Bible to suit his needs. The text (i.e., the wording) of the Bible is determined by evaluations of early copies of it in the biblical languages, by early translations, and by citations of it in the church fathers of the first several centuries. But Joe's unrestrained exaltation of himself, a vanity in him obviously adored by the Mormon establishment, enables him to, in his mind, correct the Bible. What counts is what Joe says the Bible says. The entire evidence of the ancient copies, ancient translations, and ancient citations of it must bow to the inerrancy of Joe the prophet. But why? Oh, that's right. Joe said so, and Joe is never ever wrong.

Missing Books of the Bible?

Mormons make much over the fact that books are mentioned in the Bible which are not found in the Bible. These books include "The Book of the Wars of the Lord" (Numbers 21:14), the Book of Jasher" (Joshua 10:13), "The Acts of Solomon" (1 Kings 11:41), and the Book of Iddo the Seer" (2 Chronicles 12:15). Mormons call such books "Lost Scripture."[13] But wait! Scripture? Where does the Bible call Iddo or Jasher "Scripture"? Where are the Acts of Solomon" or "The Book of the Wars of the Lord" even cited in the prophets of Israel? Where does Matthew or John or Paul tell their readers to base their beliefs on such books?

So, why would Mormons wish to claim that there are books lost from the Bible? I suspect the motive to be to induce one to be open to the possibility that the book of Mormon and the

Pearl of Great Price are additional scripture beyond the Bible. But, should we think, for example, that because Paul referenced a Greek poet (Acts 17:28), that the apostle, therefore, understood this poet's writings to be scripture? Likewise, the Bible can mention various books known to its original readers, but that is no evidence that those books are inspired scripture. Thus, these books mentioned in the Bible do not provide Mormons with any evidence to justify their belief that their other sacred books are scripture.

Doctrines Removed From the Bible?

Another ploy to downgrade the authority of the Bible is the Mormon claim that "many important points touching the salvation of men, had been taken from the Bible or lost before it was compiled."[14] As JF Smith avers, "The Bible as we have it today is very deficient."[15] But again, where is the evidence for this claim? There is none. Examine the ancient copies and translations of the Bible; these show that the Mormon assertion is fallacious and ridiculous. But the Mormons need to aver this in order to justify adding many unbiblical doctrines to their faith. If you are a Mormon, try to give convincing proof that "many important points touching the salvation of men" were removed from the Bible. That is, provide more proof than Mormons asserting that.

Review questions on Introduction

1. What are three sources which show that Smith's "Inspired Version" of the Bible contains mistakes?

2. Compare Joe Smith's role in Mormonism with the role of New Testament prophets.

3. How does Roman 7:2 refute a Mormon doctrine?

4. How are locations in the Bible where baptism was done contrary to Mormon practice?

5. Why is the Mormon argument over "lost books" of the Bible not convincing?

6. How does 1 Timothy 3:2 condemn Joe Smith?

7. What Mormon doctrine does 1 Corinthians 14:37 refute?

8. How does the Mormon "Reorganized Church" of Missouri disagree with the LDS of Utah over the doctrine of God?

9. What is the significance of the number 3,410?

10. Name some doctrines over which evangelicals differ and tell how evangelicals nevertheless, agree on the doctrine of God.

End notes for Introduction

1. ldsliving.com/10-reasons-you-should-be-a-Mormon. (accessed April 2021)

2. Bruce R. McConkie. *Doctrinal New Testament Commentary vol 3*. (Salt Lake: Bookcraft,1973), 25.

3. Bruce R. McConkie. *Mormon Doctrine*. (Salt Lake: Bookcraft, 1879), 117.

4. *Gospel Principles* (Salt Lake: published by the Church of Jesus Christ of Latter- Day Saints, 1997), 256.

5. McConkie. *Mormon Doctrine*, 623, 624.

6. *Gospel Principles*, 49.

7. Genesis 50:30, 33 in Joseph Smith's New Translation of the Bible. These verses say that a great prophet will come whose name is Joseph and whose father's name is Joseph.

8. Russel F. Ralston. *Fundamental Differences*. (Independence, Mo.,: Herald House, 1960), 18-86.

9. *Gospel Principles*, 49.

10. *Doctrines and Covenants* 135:3.

11. *Joseph Smith's New Translation* (Independence, Mo.: Herald House, 1970), 115, 451.

12. David J. Ridges. *Mormon Beliefs and Doctrines Made Easier.* (Springville, Utah, 2007), 253.

13. Richard R. Hopkins. *Biblical Mormonism.* (Bountiful, Utah: Horizon Publishers, 1994), 249.

14. Robert L. Millet, ed. *LDS Beliefs* (Salt Lake: Deseret, 2011), 68.

15. Joseph Fielding Smith. *The Way to Perfection.* (Salt Lake: Deseret, 1956), 55.

GOD THE FATHER

The Father only is *Elohim?*

Mormon theology teaches that while some exalted humans can become Gods, and being Gods in Mormonism means having "all the power in heaven and on earth,"[1] there are only three Gods in the "Godhead": Father, Son, and Holy Ghost who are distinct, separate Beings.[2] I think that one of the most unprovable assertions of Mormonism, biblically speaking, is that the name *Elohim* in the Old Testament refers in particular to the Father whereas the name *Jehovah* is that of the Son. As McConkie insists, "*Elohim* is the exalted name-title of God the eternal Father." And, why must we believe that? Oh, because of a "Doctrinal Exposition by the First Presidency and the Twelve."[3] And, as we've seen above, these are never to be questioned. Mormon prophets, the reader will remember, are never ever to be doubted.

However, recalling that the New King James Version translates *Elohim* as "God" and *Jehovah* as "LORD," it does not require much reading in the Old Testament to discern that the two are one and the same Being:

The LORD God made the earth" (Genesis 2:4); "sacrifice unto the LORD our God" (Exodus 5:3); "I am the LORD your God" (Leviticus 18:4); "The LORD my God" (Numbers 23:18); "The LORD He is God" (Deuteronomy 4:35); "the name of the LORD thy God" (Joshua 9:9); "O LORD God remember me" (Judges 16:28) ....and so forth all through the Old Testament!

In the Bible *Jehovah* (LORD) is *Elohim!* Rejecting this teaching is a solid example of how Mormons deceive their people by misrepresenting the clear doctrines of the Scriptures. The Mormon goal is to argue for there being multiple Gods by unbiblically distinguishing between *Elohim* and *Jehovah*. Again, I do not imagine that my lucid data will convince any Mormon to question his or her "inerrant" prophets. As soon as one is convinced that Mormon prophets cannot be challenged, then it makes no difference what the Bible, itself, actually says.

The Father is Spatial?

Look at what the Bible teaches about the divine omnipresence. "Whither shall I flee from Thy presence" (Psalm 139:7). "Am I a God at hand, saith Jehovah, and not a God afar off?" (Jeremiah 23:23). "Do I not fill heaven and earth?" (Jeremiah 23:24) "The heavens and the heaven of heavens cannot contain Thee. (1 Kings 8:27) In Him we live and move and have our being." (Acts 17:28) "That He might fill all things." (Ephesians 4:10). The reader will please note that these Scriptures do not say that it is merely God's power or influence which is everywhere. The

Bible says that God, Himself, is everywhere. How else could He, Himself, fill heaven and earth?

By the way, the Hebrew word for "fill" (mala) as in Jeremiah 23:24 is used to indicate that the thing itself is filling not its power or influence: Genesis 42:25, "fill their sacks with grain." The grain itself is filling. 1 Kings 18:33, "fill four water pots with water." The water itself is filling. Proverbs 1:13, "fill our houses with spoil." The spoil itself is filling. In these examples, it is the thing itself that is filling not its influence. So, when Jeremiah 23:23 states that God fills (*mala*) heaven and earth, I take this to mean that God, Himself, is filling—not merely His power. So, why would Mormons deny this? Oh, that's right, Joe Smith said that God is spatial as He is a big man. And, Joe is never, ever wrong!

One should also remember our Lord's own promise, "I am with you always." How could this be true were He not omnipresent? Jesus' disciples today are found everywhere on earth. And, Jesus is with each one of them wherever they are. So, how could our Lord in His divine nature be spatially limited? As one so much greater in erudition and accomplishment than I, by the grace given him, once wrote, "Jesus Christ came down to earth without ever leaving heaven."

And this omnipresence is true of the Father as well. For the inspired John has recorded that the Father, Himself, will make His home with us. (John 14:23). Believers are the temples of God. (1 Corinthians 3:16, 17) But how could God be spatially confined to one place, if He is with and dwells in believers all over the world?

And, that is why I am dissatisfied with Ludlow's explanation. Ludlow opines,

> Since Latter-day Saints believe that God the Father and God the Son are gloriously embodied Persons, they do not believe them to be bodily omnipresent. They do affirm rather that their power is immanent "in all and through all things." [4]

But why should Ludlow teach this depleted dogma of God's perfection? Ah yes, it is because his inerrant prophet Joe has asserted that "God ...is an exalted man."[5] So, if God the Father is a man, He must not be omnipresent. Likewise, most wonderful prophet number two, Brigham Young, declared that God the Father has a body with parts the same as you or I have."[6] So, one might ask, how do Mormons explain Numbers 23:19, "God is not a man." Oh, that verse must mean that God is not an earthly man because He is exalted. But the verse does not include such a qualification does it! The Bible says that God is not a man, but Mormon prophets say God is a man. Which will you believe?

But, wait Bill, how do you explain verses which describe God as having body parts?

The Father has body parts?

God "makes the clouds His chariot." (Psalm 104:3) So how should we interpret this verse? Should we envision that our

God while seated on a cloud is floating around the world in the sky sort of like Santa Clause in his chariot who is pulled by reindeer all through the atmosphere? Shall we imagine a God with all of our body parts-- remember Young above-- luxuriously reclining on white clouds while calmly drifting around the world and thus keeping track of His creatures? I think that most of us would rather understand Psalm 104:3 as indicating the greatness of God (see verse 1:"O Lord my God, you are very great") not the humanness of God which is riding about from place to place. But in Mormonism, the distinction between what is human and what is God is blurred. "Gods and humans are the same species of being, but at different stages of development." (Thus says Robinson in Ludlow, 197)

So, in my opinion, Psalm 104:3 is instead to be understood as an anthropomorphism which is a literary figure wherein human qualities to are ascribed to God. And, when Exodus 15:8 states, "With the blast of your nostrils the waters were gathered together," I doubt that Moses wishes his readers to picture God bending over and vigorously blowing immense, powerful winds though His nose. It is not proof that God has a nose. And when Exodus 9:3 says "the hand of the LORD will be on your cattle," I do not believe that God wanders around touching every person's cows. It is not proof that God has hands. And when Isaiah 66:1 describes the earth as God's footstool, that is not proof either that God has gigantic feet. But how can we understand God being omnipresent if He is visible?

The Father is visible?

The Bible says that God has been seen. For example, Jacob is said to have wrestled with God "until the breaking of day" and God could not prevail over Jacob. Jacob was stronger or more skilled? Perhaps Jacob was highly trained in mixed martial arts? Or, did the omnipotent God perhaps get too tired to continue? Afterward, Jacob said, "I have seen God face to face." (Genesis 32) The description of this event has an unusual feature. God could not out wrestle Jacob?! This is surprising given that God is thought to possess unlimited power. "God has all power." (Ether 3:4) Could it be that this appearance of God in weakness was not God as He really is?

Another who is said to have seen God is Moses, "The LORD spoke to Moses face to face." (Exodus 33:11) But then in the very same Book and in the very same chapter, God states to Moses, "You cannot see My face; for no man shall see Me and live." (33:20). Instead, verse 23 tells us that Moses saw God's "back." It seems that in some manner God has been visible, but could such occurrences be best understood as human-like personifications of God not God as He really is. Therefore, given such confusing narratives, I search for some definitive word about whether God in His very Person and true nature can be seen. It is not my belief that the Bible contradicts itself.

And I believe I have found it in 1 John 4:12, "No one has seen God at any time." This statement is by an apostle who was said by our Lord to be one of the recipients of "all truth." (John 16:13) John would surely have been aware of the several Old Testament references which in some manner depict seeing

God. So, I think I am correct that here the apostle means seeing God as God really is. 1 John 4:12 seems to be uncompromising in its exclusion of anyone seeing God truly as He is. But Mormons have an answer to this text too.

You see, the Bible is mistranslated here! Joe the inerrant prophet, who by the way, was no expert in the biblical languages, corrects the Bible by adding to this verse, saying, under inspiration you understand, no one has seen God "except them who believe."7(my emphasis) The reader of my small book should be alerted to the fact that there is no evidence that John wrote the latter part of this verse as Joe's "Inspired Version" has it. Our Lord Jesus promised that John would receive "all truth," yet Joe the inerrant prophet feels qualified to edit John's writing. Joe is greater than John, you see! This evidences that Mormons try to prove their doctrine by changing the Bible.

Of course, there are other related texts too. John 6:46, "Not that anyone has seen the Father, except He who is from God; He has seen the Father." But who is the One from God who has seen the Father? As our blessed Lord proclaimed of Himself, "I came forth from the Father" (John 16:48). He is the only one who has seen the Father!

In fact, the Bible elsewhere says Jesus Christ is the only one ever to have seen the Father, "No one has seen God at any time. The only begotten Son, who is in the bosom of the Father, He has declared Him." (John 1:18) How many have seen the Father? Many? Nope! A few? Nope! Joe Smith? Nope! But Joe's "corrected" translation (Joseph Smith's New Translation of the Bible[7]) fixes John 1:18 to read, "no man hath seen God at any time, except he hath borne record of the Son." Mormons change the writings of the Bible's teaching in order to substantiate Joe Smith's blatant, delusional tenets. How can anyone not see the so very obvious Mormon deception?

The Father is the Supreme God?

Robinson, a Mormon, writes,

> The divine Son and the Holy Spirit are subordinate to the Father and dependent on their oneness with Him for their divinity. They cannot stand alone; they are God only as they are one with the Father. If their oneness with the Father should cease, so would their divinity.[8]

By "oneness," Robinson means not a unity in Being as he declares, the divine Persons are "separate Beings with separate and individual bodies."[9] It is true that some evangelicals subscribe to the tenet of the Son's eternal role subordination.[10] However, no evangelical believes that the Son or the Holy Spirit is of a difference essence than the Father.

Yes, there were those in the formative centuries of the church who subordinated the Son's Person to that of the Father due to believing that the Father provided His divine nature to the Son. A case in point is Origen of the third century who exposits the Greek of John 1:1 in this manner:

He (John) adds the article when the name of
God refers to the uncreated cause of all things,
and omits it when the Logos is named God.
(Christ) is made God by His participation in His
(the Father's) divinity...not possessing that in
Himself, but by His being with the Father. (Origin's Commentary on John II:2)

And so, yes, in the writing of this third century believer we
have one whose doctrine appears to correlate in some way to
Mormon Christology that the Son is somehow lesser in deity
than is the Father because, Origen notes, the Greek article does
not modify Christ in John 1:1. As I will later show, though, unlike Mormon doctrine, Origen insists that the Father and Son
share the identical essence. But Origen believed that the Father
was the Originator of the Son's divine essence. However, it is
hermeneutically unfortunate that Origen bases his doctrine
on the Son's receiving divinity on the absence of an article (i.e.,
"the") for in the very same book (John 20:28) the Son is called
"the God of me" with the article (ho theos mou) and so it is with
Paul (Titus 2:13). Moreover, even in John chapter one when
"God" clearly refers to the Father, the noun repeatedly occurs
without the article (1:6, 12, 18).

There are, of course, New Testament references which say
that the Father is greater in some manner than the Son. But, in
my view, these concern the relationships of God to creation—
where each divine Person has chosen to act in unique ways--
or in addition, these often relate to the human nature of Jesus
not to His divinity. One of such is John 14:28, "My Father is

greater than I." However, could we please remember that this saying followed the divine Son "becoming flesh" (John 1:14). It followed the eternal Christ assuming the nature of a bond servant (Philippians 2:7), and it was in that nature that He began to be obedient (2:8). It followed Jesus being made like His brethren (Hebrews 2:9, 14). It is in Christ's human nature, therefore, that He is less than the Father in authority, I contend, not in His deity. The ancient Greeks believed in ranking their gods, and so do the modern Mormons.

So, in my view, as the Son as God and the Father are equal in essence, how then can the Son's obedience on earth to the Father be explained? In my opinion, clearly, the obedience of Jesus to God the Father occurs in Christ's human nature only. That Christ at times experienced through His humanity only is indicated by His, for example, falling asleep in a boat (Mark 4:38) and dying. I don't think God takes naps or dies. Therefore, I think texts like John 8:29, "I always do those things that please Him," have Jesus' human nature only as their referent not His divine nature which is "equal to God" (Philippians 2:6).

That the New Testament alludes to the acts of Jesus, at times, distinctly as one or the other nature in Christ is clearly set forth further in Jesus being tired in John 4:6 but holding the universe together in Colossians 1:17 or knowing everything (John 16:30, 21:17) but not knowing somethings (Mark 13:32). In other words, the one Person of Christ specifically experiences and acts, at times, through just one of His natures.

And, in my opinion, it is in His humanity, which He assumed from being born of Mary, that our Lord is role subordinate to the Father. Mormons cannot countenance this doctrine as it is contrary to their belief that Gods and humans are the same race. So, they, instead teach that Christ has only one nature and in that one nature He is less in essence than the Father. In the fourth century the framers of the Nicene creed instead enunciated the position that Son of God is "one essence (substance) with the Father." That, universally, is now the evangelical view. But is it biblical?

The Mormon position that the Father is different in Being from the Son requires that the Son who is *Jehovah* in Mormon thought is a second God besides the Father. But were the Bible to teach that Jehovah is the only God, then Mormon theology is incorrect. And, the Bible certainly does conclusively proclaim that only *Jehovah* is God:

> Thus says the LORD (i.e., *Jehovah*) Besides Me there is no God. (Isaiah 44:6) I am the LORD, and there is no other; There is no God besides Me. (Isaiah 45:6) (my emphasis)

The Mormon doctrine of God thus is shown to be contrary to the teachings of Isaiah. Once again, the Bible refutes Mormon doctrine. But if you are a Mormon, please prove from the Bible that *Jehovah* is a different God than *Elohim*. One cannot prove that, and the consequence is that Mormonism teaches an unbiblical doctrine of God.

The Father is not eternal as He has a Father?

McConkie bloviates that his precious Joe the prophet reasoned that "God the Father of Jesus Christ had a Father."[11] Can this teaching be reconciled with the Bible? Does the Bible anywhere say that God our Father had a Father or that Christ has a grandpappy God? A Mormon may respond that it matters not whether the Bible teaches that because the inerrant prophet Joe taught it. And, ummm we know Joe is a prophet because the 30th and 33rd verses, which Joe in his "inspired" translation, without evidence of their originality, inserted into Genesis 50 say he is a prophet. But should one instead rather observe the Bible's teaching about God, let's note the words of the Psalmist, "From everlasting to everlasting You are God." (90:2) But if God (*Elohim*) has always been God, how could He have been sired by a Father?

The Father is mutable?

Evangelicals, therefore on the basis of Psalm 90:2 and also on other biblical evidence (e.g., Isaiah 41:4 and Revelation 1:8) affirm that God eternally is God. He has always been God. Therefore, He does not change. Mormons, however, assert that God does change. Millet, for example, informs his readers that the evangelical doctrine of God's immutability is "adapted from Greek thought (my emphasis)."[12] Now, I've just provided immediately above, verses in the Bible which say that God eternally has been God. And, I now offer more general biblical proof that God does not change:

> Of old You laid the foundation of the earth. and
> the heavens are the work of Your hand. ...and
> they will be changed. But You are the same.
> (Psalm 102: 25, 26, 27) "For I am the LORD, I do
> not change. (Malachi 3:6)

Let the reader note that these biblical texts regarding God's immutability are from Hebrew Scriptures not, as Millet avows, from the Greeks.

However, since Millet introduces the topic of supposed Greek influence on evangelical theology, let's compare ancient Greek religion with modern Mormonism. As an aid for my doing this, I will reference Richard Buxton, Professor of Greek language and literature at the University of Bristol.[13]Let's note some points Buxton makes about the gods of the Greeks:

1. The gods of Greece were often portrayed as human like in form as is demonstrated, for example, in the sculpture of Zeus and Hera circa 470 B.C. located in Selinus, Italy.[14]

And, in Mormonism, the divinities in the Godhead are also human. God is simply an exalted man.

2. There was a plurality of deities in the Greek pantheon, including among others, such as Poseidon, Demeter, Athene, and Ares.[15]

And, in Mormonism also there is also more than one God. As the prophet Brigham Young expressed in his Discourses (7:33), "How many Gods (his capital) there are, I do not know."

3. To the Greeks, Zeus was the father of both gods and mortals.[16]

And, in Mormonism God the Father begets all humans as "spirit children" who then may become Gods themselves. By the way, again, Mormons are not adverse about capitalizing the "G" in Gods when the noun has humans as its reference. As evidence note Joe Smith in the King Follet Discourse, "You have got to learn how to be Gods yourselves." So, if Joe tells others to learn to be Gods, one can assume that Joe considered himself to be, or soon to be, a God!

4. To the Greeks, gods had sex with mortals. Apollo, for example, bargained with Cassandra for her virginity.[17]

And, in Mormonism, as discussed below, God the Father took Mary as His wife.

5. To the Greeks, gods can change. There is the story, for example, of Ouranos undergoing bodily changes by having his private parts severed.[18]

And, in Mormonism, as seen above, God the Father also changes "growing up" from "spirit child" to become the chief Member of the Godhead.

6. To the Greeks, gods have not existed from eternity. Even Zeus was conceived by two titans.[19]

And, in Mormonism the Gods are also not eternal as they too originated by being born as "spirit children." Even God the Father, as shown above, had a Father!

7. To the Greeks, gods are spatially confined in one location at a time. So, Typhon who warred with Zeus, dwelt in a cave in southern Asia Minor. [20]

And, in Mormonism too the Gods are not omnipresent.

8. The Greeks gods sometimes had wives. Hera, recall, was married to Zeus. [21]

And, in Mormonism God the Father, as discussed below, has His own wife or wives.

9. To the Greeks, gods are subordinate to other gods. Even Zeus' sovereignty was limited by the influences of other divinities.[22]

And, in Mormonism, God the Son is subordinate to God the Father. God is subject to God. Imagine that!

10. To the Greeks, the society of the gods were like those of human beings. Zeus was the head of the family of the Olympians. [23]

And, according to Mormonism, in heaven, exalted humans who have become Gods exist in family units as does God the Father, Hiumself.

Clearly, one can see that the deities of Mormonism bear marked similarities to the gods of ancient Greece. Perhaps those, as Millet, who live in glass houses should not throw stones!

The Father has a God-wife?

In contradiction to any biblical statement or early Christian church tenet which I've encountered, including those of the first century apostolic fathers, thought to have been disciples of the apostles, like Clement of Rome, Ignatius, and Polycarp, I never have come across anything remotely like the absurd Mormon fiction that God the Father has a God-wife or wives. Yet, that God the Father has wives is taught by Joe the "prophet's" designated teacher of Mormonism, Apostle Orson Pratt. But Pratt denies that these God-wives should be worshipped:

> But if we have a heavenly Mother as well as a heavenly Father, is it not right that we should worship the Mother of our spirits as well as the Father? No; for the Father of our spirits is the head of His household, and His wives and children are required to yield the most perfect obedience to their great Head.[24]

Nor is this unbiblical teaching of a Mother God confined to just one Mormon. For Millet cites an LDS church president who asserts,

> Man, as a spirit was begotten and born of heavenly parents...all men and women are in the similitude of the universal Father and Mother, and are literally the sons and daughters of deity.[25]

So, do you know how many times the Bible says that we were spirit children of a Mother God? Is it lots of times? Nope! OK, is it a few times? Nope! Just once then? Nope. The Bible never says that we have a Mother God. It is a pure Mormon fabrication. Need I give any further evidence that the Mormon doctrine of deity errs grievously? Or, if you are a Mormon, please refer me to where the Bible anywhere says there is a "Mother God."

Yet, the teaching of our being heavenly "spirit children" before acquiring bodies permeates Mormon literature. *Doctrines of the Gospel*, for example teaches that we were spirit beings in heaven birthed by exalted parents and we dwelt for ages in that pre-mortal state. There we developed characteristics and became, or did not become worthy. We lived in a perfectly arranged society in heaven Eventually we received bodies in order to attain the goal of perfection.[26]

The Father became Husband to Mary?

Another unique teaching of Mormonism is that God the Father became husband to Mary and sired in her Jesus our Savior. Turning again to Orson Pratt, who was an original member of the quorum of the Twelve Apostles, we read this unholy verbiage:

> Therefore, the Father and Mother of Jesus, according to the flesh, must have been associated together in the capacity of Husband and Wife... God having created all men and women, had

the most perfect right to do with His own creation, according to His holy will and pleasure: He had the lawful right to over shadow the Virgin Mary in the capacity of a husband, and beget a Son, although she was espoused to another...Whether God the Father gave Mary to Joseph for a time only, or instead for time and eternity, we are not informed. It may be that He intended after the resurrection to again take her as a one of His own wives ... .[27]

This is just amazing theology: Mary may have been passed from Joseph to God, then back to Joseph, then, back again, to God? This is ridiculous and is sacrilege. But lest we think that Pratt's heresy of God having a sexual relationship with Mary goes unrepeated in Mormon literature, observe that McConkie declares that "Christ was begotten by an Immortal Father in the same way (my emphasis) that mortal men are begotten by mortal fathers."[28] In the same way!! The Mormon misconception that God is a man nowhere is more explicitly shown than in the Mormons teaching that God the Father had celestial sex with Mary. Mormons set no boundaries in their attempt to make God like man. They do create God in their own image.

The Father is Adam?

Mormons have invented a number of unbiblical teachings about Adam. Adam administered the principles and ordinances of the Gospel and he is Michael the Arch Angel. He participates in governing the kingdom of heaven. He may have restored the power of immortality to his descendants.[29] None of this, of course, is in or even hinted at in the Bible. But does this matter to Mormons? Not at all! Adam is the presiding high priest (under Christ) over the earth for all time. Adam received a state and power second only to Christ. He is the head of all gospel dispensations.[30] None of this, of course is in or is even hinted at in the Bible. But does this matter to Mormons? Not at all! Adam participated in the creation of the world as well.[31] That also is not in the Bible. Does this matter to Mormons? Not at all!

However, these assertions above about Adam pale before Brigham Young's "inspired" teaching. Let's recall that in Mormon belief the president of the LDS "has the right to revelation for the entire church...and, will never be allowed to lead the church astray."[32] But I refer the reader to John David Berger's "The Adam-God Doctrine."[33] Here one is provided with indisputable proof that Young taught and was understood by his Mormon hearers as teaching that Adam is God.

In April of 1852 Young speaking to a session of the general conference avowed that "Adam is our Father and God, and the only God with whom we have to do." Both Hosea Stout and Samuel H. Rodgers who heard Young that day, acknowledged in writing that the (infallible) LDS president asserted that doctrine. In 1870 Elder George Cannon concurred with Young saying that "Father Adam is our God and Father." Also, in 1870 did apostle Orson Hyde. It is true that today Mormons try to argue that Young's words are misrepresented or are not LDS doctrine. But, Young is deemed a prophet-president, and

Mormons, as said above, claim those like Young have the power of revelation for the entire church!

Review questions for chapter 1

1. Define anthropomorphism and tell how is it demonstrated in Exodus 9:3.

2. Explain John 6:46.

3. What Mormon doctrine does 1 Kings 8:27 refute?

4. Tell three ways the gods of ancient Greece were like the Mormon Gods.

5. How does the Bible show that *Elohim* is the same God as *Jehovah*?

6. What have Mormons taught about Mary's "marriages"?

7. How does the Old Testament usage of the Hebrew word *mala* contradict Mormon theology?

8. What Mormon teaching does Malachi 3:6 refute?

9. How did Joe Smith change 1 John 4:12?

10. In your opinion, what are the three most fallacious Mormon doctrines about Adam?

End Notes on Chapter 1

1. Bruce R. McConkie. *Mormon Doctrine.* (Salt Lake: Bookcraft, 1979), 257.

2. David J. Ridges. *Mormon Beliefs and Doctrines Made Easier.* (Springfield, Utah: CFI, 2007), 121.

3. McConkie. *Mormon Doctrine, 224.*

4. Daniel H. Ludlow, ed. *Jesus Christ and His Gospel.* (Salt Lake: Deseret, 1992),369.

5. Joseph Smith. *King Follet Discourse.*

6. Brigham Young. *Discourses,*1:50.

7. Joseph Smith. *New Translation of the Bible.* (Independence, Mo. : Herald House, 1970),512.

8. Stephen E. Robinson and Craig L. Blomberg. *How Wide the Divide?* (Downer's Grove, Ill.: Intervarsity, 1977), 132.

9. *Ibid.,* 130.

10. Bruce A. Ware and John Stark, eds. *One God in Three Persons.* (Wheaton, Ill.: Crossways, 2015).

11. Bruce R. McConkie. *Doctrinal New Testament, vol III.* (Salt Lake: Bookcraft, 1973),437.

12. Robert L. Millet. *Getting at the Truth.* (Salt Lake: Deseret, 2004), 119.

13. Richard Buxton. *The Complete World of Greek Mythology*. (London: Thames and Hudson), 2004

14. *Ibid., 71*.

15. *Ibid., 69*.

16. *Ibid*.

17. *Ibid., 100*.

18. *Ibid.,78*.

19. *Ibid., 47*.

20. *Ibid., 49*.

21. *Ibid., 71*.

22. *Ibid., 69*.

23. *Ibid., 68*.

24. Orson Pratt. *The Seer*. (U.S.A.: Eborn,2009), 159.

25. Robert L. Millet, ed. *LDS Beliefs*. (Salt Lake: Deseret, 2011), 441.

26. *Doctrines of the Gospel, Student Manual, Religion 430, 431, page 14*.

27. Pratt, 158.

28. McConkie, 549.

29. Millet, 20, 21.

30. McConkie, 16, 18.

31. Ridges, 6.

32. *Principles of the Gospel.* (Salt Lake: published by the Church of the Latter-Day Saints, 1997), 48, 49.

33. David John Beurger. "The Adam-God Doctrine." University of Illinois Press. lstor.org/stable/pdf45225052.pdf. (accessed May, 2021)

GOD THE SON

The Son has a different essence than the Father?

While evangelicals maintain that the unity in essence among the Persons in the Trinity is due to These Persons comprising only one God, Mormons deny that the Father, Son, and Holy Spirit are essentially the same Being. This LDS doctrine is necessary for their teaching of the plurality of Gods. Mormons argue that evangelicals are wrong to accept the positions of fourth and fifth century Christian belief statements (Nicene and Chalcedon) on the unity of God's being.

Robinson explains why he and other Mormons reject the doctrine that the Persons in the Godhead are the same in essence or substance. It is because the Nicene and Chalcedon creeds which teach that doctrine are perversions, he claims, of a more primitive Christian teaching.[1] These creeds, Robinson claims, do not concur with the earlier Christian doctrine of the church which distinguishes between the essence of the Father and the essence of the Son. The Nicene Creed of 381 states that Christ is "one substance (essence) with the Father" and the Chalcedon Creed in 451 states that Christ is "consubstantial (coessential) with the Father."[2] But this is rejected by Mormons.

But do these creedal statements contradict the earlier teaching of the Church in regard to the unity of substance existing between the divine Persons? As Mormons insist that they do, let Mormon apologist provide excerpts from the early church fathers which teach that the divine essence of the Son differs from the Father's essence. One who has read the ante-Nicene church fathers, i.e., those writing before creed of Nicaea, will be aware that up to near 200 A.D. the issue of there being a common substance among the divine Persons was not broached in their writings. Read Clement of Rome, Ignatius, Justin Martyr, Irenaeus and others to see that omission. But when the nature between the Son and the Father began to be seriously discussed, the church fathers Athenagorus, Tertullian, and then Origen addressed it. And, these all wrote long before the Nicene Creed was framed. Let's note what each taught about the unity between the Father and the Son.

As I briefly comment on these three early Christians, I'd like to accomplish two objectives. I wish to show that these three, pre-Nicene Christian theologians taught that there is but one essence between the Father and the Son as They are one and the same God. And I also want to show that these early believers did not teach some other doctrines about God and Christ which Mormonism enthusiastically proclaim today. The Mormon gods clearly are not a restoration of early Christian teaching.

Athenagoras in his attempt to demonstrate that Christians are not atheists had a strong motive to define the Christian God. He who died in 177 A.D. barely scratched the surface of God's Trinity in unity, but he wrote in stark contradiction to the fundamental Mormon doctrine of there being many Gods. In an age when many deities were worshipped, Athenagoras taught that there is only one God.[3] (*That contradicts Mormonism!) But as the Father, the Son, and the Holy Spirit each is God[4], yet since there is only one God, there is a <u>unity between the Three</u>.[5] This church father died two hundred years before the Nicene Creed was written. But his doctrine of the three Persons in one God is certainly not in conflict with it!

Now let's look at Tertullian who died in 220 A.D. many decades before the Nicene Creed was composed. Tertullian's lengthy *Prescription Against Heretics*, which includes condemnations of modern Mormon unbiblical tenets about God, affirms the unity between the Father and the Son and that unity is evidenced by his declaration that there is "one only God" (*This contradicts Mormonism) not three or many.[6] Tertullian, in fact, refutes common arguments used today by Mormons in their attempt to disprove the oneness of God. He rejects that "He judges among the gods" (Psalm 82:1) and "Ye are gods" (Psalm 82:6) are evidences of a plurality of Gods.[7] (*These opinions contradict Mormonism)

And this one God, Tertullian insists, "has no human characteristics."[8] (*This contradicts Mormonism.) God is not physical. [9] (*This contradicts Mormonism.) The Persons who compose the Trinity furthermore, are <u>one in substance</u> and power.[10]

Tertullian repeatedly states that the Son and Spirit are of "the Father's own substance."[11] Clearly, Tertullian's teaching, therefore, is not contrary to the creeds of Nicaea and Chalcedon which proclaim belief in the unity of essence between the Son and the Father. Further, this ancient Christian also taught that Christ exists in two natures and that each nature retains its own properties preserved.[12] (*This contradicts Mormonism.)

Lastly, consider Origen who died in 254 long before the Nicene Creed was written. Origen in his Preface to *De Principiis* explains that he writes in an attempt to instruct those who held incorrect views about God, Christ, and the Holy Spirit. [13] He states that there is only one God not three or many.[14] (*This contradicts Mormonism) Furthermore, Origen states that God does not have a body.[15] (*This contradicts Mormonism.) The Son is eternally and everlastingly generated by the Father, and the Father cannot be seen.[16] ` (*This contradicts Mormonism). Christ has no separation from the Father.[17] There is, in fact, no dissimilarity between the Son and the Father.[18] The Word and God share one nature. The nature of deity is common to the Father and the Son.[20] And, Origen furthermore teaches that Christ has two natures a divine and a human.[21] (*This contradicts Mormonism.) I believe that I have clearly shown that the Mormon doctrine about God is not that of the early church.

The Son has only One nature?

Hopefully the reader will indulge me for interacting with this topic again even though I do that elsewhere as well. The Mormon understanding of Christ having one nature is central to their doctrines of both God and man. Robinson claims, "The theological proposition of two natures in Christ (is) an invention of the post apostolic church."[22] So, the two natures of our Lord Jesus is not found in the New Testament? But before we take up the issues of Christ's natures in the Bible, let's remind ourselves of the Mormon motivation for denying that our Lord exists in two natures and of what a nature constitutes. Mormons would have us believe that men are the same race as God. God is just an exalted man. Man can become an exalted God. To admit that Christ, who is God, has another nature which is not God would compromise these Mormon teachings.

And perhaps I can suggest what I think is a "nature." A nature is not a person; it is what a person is like. Hence evangelicals are not saying that Christ is two Persons. Rather, a nature includes the characteristics of a person: how tall he is; how strong he is, his intellectual and emotional qualities, and so forth. In my view, while one's nature affects how one interacts with the forces, options, and experiences he encounters, it is the one Person of Christ who acts and experiences through each of His natures distinctly. That is why the Gospel accounts of His life describe Christ experiencing and acting in two different ways.

Were my thinking correct, then, in my view, a nature would seem to necessarily include emotions, will, and intelligence. But these do not equal a "person;" instead they describe a person. I believe each nature in Christ possesses these faculties; He has two natures since the Incarnation. And, in my opinion, that Jesus Christ exists in two natures is demonstrated by His experiencing and acting in two wholly diverse manners in the Gospel accounts of His life.

Consider, for example, the issues of the mutability, knowledge, and suffering of Jesus in regard to the two natures in Christ. Let's do this by first referencing Mormon Scriptures on the nature of God, then the New Testament teaching about Jesus Christ, whom Mormons believe is God (in their sense of the meaning of God), and by these comparisons deduce whether Christ exists in two natures. So, we read in Mosiah 4:9 that God has all power both in heaven and earth. But, then how could Christ as God be beaten, suffer, and die (Matthew chapters 26, 27)? Does one who has all power die? We read in Doctrines and Covenants 38:2 that God knows all things. But were this true, how could Christ in His divinity grow in knowledge (Luke 2:40), learn (Hebrews 5:8), and not know some things (Mark 13:32)? We read in Mormon 9:9 that God does not change. But were this true, how can the Son mature and grow in size (Luke 2:52)? I think that the contrast between the Gospel accounts of Jesus' human limitations and experiences and the Mormon scriptures on God's nature require belief in the two natures in Christ: one nature God and the other man.

To drive this farther home, note that the New Testament teaches that Christ does not change (Hebrews 1:12), is almighty (Revelation 1:8), and knows everything (John 16:30; 21:17) How could He not change unless He exists in two natures one of which is not immutable? How could He know everything but not know somethings unless He exists in two natures one of which is not omniscient? How could He die if He is almighty unless He exists in two natures one of which lacks aseity?

But note the clear New Testament affirmations of Christ existing in two natures. In John 1:1, 14; 20:28 God became flesh. But He still is God. In Hebrews 1:12 and 2:17 we see that Christ who cannot change in His divine nature added a second nature of humanity to His Person. And, in Philippians 2:6-8 Christ who continues to exist as God ("being" in verse 6 is present tense) took a second nature which is human and in which He obeyed and died. Clearly the New Testament teaches the two natures in Christ.

The Son Was created?

Hopkins [23] has produced a remarkably inane exposition of John 1:1-3.

> In the beginning was the Word, and the Word was with God, and the Word was God. He was in the beginning with God. All things were made through Him, and without Him nothing was made that was made.

Hopkins asserts these five things:

(1) Evangelical interpretation which says that Christ was at the beginning with God is based on ignorance of Christ's eternal existence as an "intelligence." Mormons, it should be recalled, believe that before we all (including Christ) were born as a

"spirit children" in heaven, we first existed as "intelligences." But, the Bible nowhere states that we and Christ first existed as "intelligences." That is why evangelicals "are ignorant" of that. In none of the scores of Books in the Bible is it ever taught that we first existed as "intelligences"! Mormons can suppose that for thousands of years, God kept our origin hid from those who believed in Him; I cannot. "Restoring" the Gospel does not mean adding to it what never was there in the first place!

(2) The passage is saying that Christ being created as "a spirit child" was the beginning of God's creative acts. But, the Bible nowhere states that Christ was ever a "spirit child." Does that fact matter to Mormons? Ummm not at all!

(3) The passage means that Christ was with God after Christ was created. But, the Bible instead states that Christ exists from eternity. "I am the Alpha and the Omega, the Beginning and the End." (Revelation 1:8).

(4) Christ was God because He was raised to that status. But, the Bible knows nothing about Christ ever not being God. He was God before anything was created. "You Lord in the beginning" (Hebrews 1:10).

(5) All things were created after Christ was created. But, the Bible instead insists that Christ is before all things and that He created all things. "By Him all things were created...For He is before all things." (Colossians 1:16, 17) Mormons reject the clear teachings of the Bible to teach their unbiblical Christology.

The Son is the firstborn spirit child?

Hopkins[24] argues this from the Greek compound adjective *prōtotokos* as found in Colossians 1:15. Hopkins opines that as this word is from two Greek roots which in themselves mean first (*prō*) and born (*tokos*), therefore any interpretation that Christ is not the Father's "first born" is in error. But it is poor interpretation to limit our understanding of words to root meanings. Take the term "apostle" for example. It is cognate to *apostlellō* which means "I send." Yet, "apostle" as used in the New Testament generally means much more than merely being sent. It includes the ideas of being given power in church leadership and authority in guiding doctrinal development. Or, take the English word "good bye" which is a contraction of the Anglo -Saxon "God be with you." But most people saying "good bye" are not referencing God. Therefore, in my opinion, Hopkin's lexical awareness is tainted by his urgent desire to defend Mormon Christology.

Let's note that D.A. Carson, Ph.D. Cambridge University, warns against requiring that root meanings must determine word meanings.[25] Also, Arndt and Gingrich, eminent scholars of New Testament Greek deny that the word "first born" in New Testament Greek necessarily includes the idea of being born [26] as do also Michaelis[27] and Bartels.[28] Note that it is not because these experts are not Mormons that they express these opinions. While the New Testament does speak of Jesus being the first born of Mary (Matthew 1:25), the term is also used to denote other experiences besides being born: "Jesus Christ.... the first born (*prōtotokos)* from the dead." (Revelation

1:5). Jesus was not birthed by death. Christ, instead, is the first resurrected individual. He has, in that manner, i.e., being the first one, pre- eminence among those who are to be later resurrected.

So, given that the Greek term may reference being born of a parent or instead being pre- eminent, how should we understand Colossians 1:15: "He is...the first born"? Well, look at the context. Christ is over all creation (15). All things were created for Him. (16). He is before all things. (17) He is head of the church. (18) In Him God's fullness dwells. (19) The passage, therefore, is not talking about Christ being born; it is talking about Christ being pre-eminent!

But I have wondered if the Mormon doctrine of Christ being the first born "spirit child" was not influenced by the Reformation era and later Protestant Christian teaching of "eternal generation," with which many evangelicals today concur. The Belgic Confession of Faith of 1561 states "the only begotten Son of God, begotten from eternity."[29] The Westminster Confession of Faith of 1647 states that "The Son is eternally begotten of the Father."[30] The Second Helvetic Confession of 1566 states that Christ "was begotten...before all eternity"[31] And, The Articles of Religion of the Reformed Episcopal Church in America written in 1875 states that "The Son (was) begotten by the Father from everlasting."[32] Did Joe, the prophet or his followers know of the teaching of such creeds? Did they twist creedal meaning to fit their new doctrine of Christ being born as a "spirit child"?

By the way, as these creeds are not those of churches which subscribe to God being physical. By saying Christ as God was "begotten" these belief statements clearly are not implying that the physical Father sired the physical Son in a physical Mother God. What is meant by the Son's eternally being begotten is that the Father eternally supplies the Son's Person and/or His divinity with the essence of God.

These creedal confessions are much different than the Mormon doctrine. They do not say that a mother God cooperated with God the Father in the heavenly birthing of the Son. They do not say that God the Son was created by His heavenly birth. They do not say that Christ was a "spirit child." They do not say that He as a spirit child became a God by His obedience to the Gospel in heaven. Rather, they say that the Son's Person or divinity is eternally, timelessly, generated by the Father, as God, from the Father's own essence, and the manner of His generation is not explicitly defined since the Bible itself does not define it. As said, many modern evangelicals accept this doctrine but many others do not. Some of us do not see it as a biblical teaching. We are not required to conform our beliefs to such creeds or to a 19th century, supposedly infallible prophet either.

The Son is Satan's brother?

Hopkins[33]-- who because he believes that we all, including Christ and every individual, were heavenly "spirit children" of God the Father-- thinks Job 1:6 means that Satan too was a heavenly "spirit child" of God. Therefore, Satan is brother to both Christ and to us. Besides Job 1:6 Hopkins also thinks that John 20:17 and Romans 8:29, are further solid proofs that we all were pre-existent as heavenly spirit children. Let's interact with these biblical arguments individually. Were these three texts not evidence for the Mormon doctrine of "spirit children," then Hopkin's attempt to prove his belief that Satan is brother to Jesus is false. His doctrine is based on both our Lord and Satan being born of the Father as heavenly "spirit children."

But first let's briefly review this LDS teaching of "spirit children." Mormons believe that God the Father and a Mother God birthed us as the sons and daughters of deity. From the time of our spiritual birth, we lived in heaven for an infinite duration before receiving bodies, and there we by "agency" (i.e., free will) experienced probation, schooling, and progression. Satan was one of these heavenly "spirit children" but he rebelled against the Father. But others of these "spirit children" were more intelligent, obedient, and noble and these were rewarded for their obedience by being foreordained to greatness upon becoming flesh.[34] This doctrine obviously makes our present state and redemption the result not of God's grace but of the extent of our pre-existent goodness in pre-mortality.

So, with this background, should we not inquire as to how much of this Mormon teaching is indicated by the three biblical texts which Hopkins employs in an effort to prove that Satan is Jesus' brother? If these do not evidence our, and Satan's, pre-existence as heavenly "spirit children" who obeyed or did not obey God the Father, then Hopkins has failed to defend his position.

(1) "spirit children" in Job 1:6?

> Now there was a day when the sons of God
> came to present themselves before the LORD,
> and Satan also came among them.

It has been the common Jewish understanding that these "sons of God" are angels. For example, see Josephus in Antiquities, Apocryphon which is a Dead sea Scroll, and the Septuagint translation of the Hebrew into Greek which in Job 1:6 reads, *"hoi aggeloi tou theou"* that is, "the angels of God." And, Mormons agree that Satan can be understood as being an angel.[35] But, angels are nowhere said in the Bible to have been born of God the Father or to have been "spirit children." Angels rather would be included among the "principalities or powers" which were created through Christ. (Colossians 1:16) If the Son of God were responsible for their creation, then He is not a sibling to them. Thus, Job 1:6 is not evidence that Satan is Jesus' brother.

(2) "spirit children" in John 20:17?

> Jesus said to her, "Do not cling to Me, for I have
> not ascended to My Father; but go to My breth-
> ren and say to them, I am ascending to My Fa-
> ther and your Father, and to My God and your
> God."

However, "being like His brethren" meant Christ becoming human (Hebrews 2:14, 17) not being a "spirit child" in heaven with them. And, those who obey God on earth are Christ's brethren not those who were obedient "spirit children" in heaven. (Mark 3:33) John 20:17 does not indicate that we all were born of God in heaven where we lived for a long duration and obeyed or did not obey. The text furthermore says nothing about Satan's origin. Therefore, John 20:17 fails to evidence that Satan is Jesus' brother.

(3) Romans 8:29 and "spirit children."

> For whom He foreknew, He also predestined to
> be conformed to the image of His Son, that He
> might be the first born among many brethren.

However, this text does not stipulate that God foreknew these because He became acquainted with them in their heavenly sojourn as "spirit children." What Mormons leave out of their attempt to substantiate their doctrine of pre-mortality is the biblical teaching of the prescience of God. God declares "the end from the beginning" and "from ancient times things that are not yet done." For He has spoken it and will bring it to pass; He has purposed it and will also it (Isaiah 46:10, 11). The foreknowledge of God is not based on what He has learned about our heavenly goodness but on what He has decreed. He knows ahead of time what will occur because He has planned, that is predestined, all things. (Ephesians 1:11) Observe that no reference to Satan being a heavenly "spirit child" born of God the Father is alluded to in Romans 8:29. So again, Hopkins' argument fails because his doctrine plainly is not biblical.

The Son, after His being born a spirit child eventually became a God?

Millet [36] asserts that "As a premortal spirit, Jehovah (i.e., Christ) grew in knowledge and power to the point where he became 'like unto God.' " To evidence this, Millet refers his readers to the Mormon Scriptures D&C, Moses, Mosiah, and 3 Nephi. But he cites no verse from the Bible as proof. Likewise, another Mormon theologian, McConkie, avers that Christ by devotion to the truth achieved intelligence which ranked Him as a God while yet in His pre-existent state. [37] Neither does this writer supply his readers with any biblical text which says that Christ was a heavenly "spirit child" who became a God. I do not see how anyone could deny that some Mormon teachings about our Lord Jesus Christ simply are not found in the Bible.

But, is there anything in the Bible which contradicts that Christ began as a "spirit child" and developed properties and powers which transformed Him into a God? First note, as above, that Christ is never called a "spirit child" who learned. Second, the Bible states that Christ always was God. John 1:1, "In the beginning...the Word was God." Third, Christ's divinity does not change, Hebrews 1:12, "You are the same." That suggests that He did not slowly grow into Godhood. These biblical evidences are a clear contradiction to the Mormon doctrine of the pre-existent Christ progressing into a God.

The Son as God is subject to the Father?

It is Mormon doctrine that the Father is the "supreme God."[38] I take this to mean that since those in the Godhead are thought by Mormons to be separate Beings,[39] that in Mormon theology both the Father's authority and also His nature are greater than that of the Son. Christ is seen as subordinate in role by Mormons because they also believe that He is a different God and is the Father's "spirit son." Some evangelicals as well teach the eternal role subordination of the Son, but none aver His essential subordination.

A number of New Testament texts have been used to indicate that the Son is eternally under the Father's authority. But do such Scriptures really teach that? Let's look at some. But first note that a recurring theme in my interpretations is that I believe that Christ exists in two natures, human and divine, that Christ experiences and acts differently in each nature, and that the meaning of some of these verses pivots on deciding which nature is the referent in the text.

John 5:18, 19.

> Then Jesus answered and said to them, "Most assuredly I say to you, the Son can do nothing of Himself, but what He sees the Father do; for whatever He does, the Son also does in like manner. For the Father loves the Son, and shows Him all things that He Himself does; and He will show Him greater works than these that you may marvel.

I am aware of three different understandings of this text. One is that God the Son only has delegated authority from the Father. Were one believing that God is the boss of God, then that interpretation could be deemed acceptable. A second view is that only Christ's human nature is the referent. That the Father will later show the Son more works, may put a temporal meaning on the passage which better alludes to the Son incarnate. That the Son will learn more from the Father in the future also could be an evidence that Jesus's humanity is the subject since in His deity He knows everything from eternity.

The third view is that the unity between the Persons in God makes the exclusive and divided activity of one of the Persons impossible. That is thought to be why the Son as God can do nothing by Himself. What the Father does, the Son also does. Were this understanding of the text correct, then John 5:18, 19 is actually an evidence of the equality of the Son with the Father. It also is evidence of the unity of the Father and the Son. We can recall, for example, that all Three are involved in both creation and salvation. One might reply, "Well did not only the Son die for our sins?" But, it may be countered that Christ's dying was confined to His humanity as divinity cannot die because it cannot change. As even Mormon 9:19 says, God "changeth not; if so He would cease to be God." Dying would be a changing, right? But God the Son agreed, it seems ("He humbled Himself," Philippians 2:8) , to become man for our salvation. Of the three views, it would seem that the second, that Jesus' humanity is the referent, is best supported by the context which informs that the Son as man learns from the Father in time.

John 6:38

> For I have come down from Heaven, not to do
> My own will, but the will of Him who sent Me.

One issue in interpreting this verse is whether each "Person" in God has a distinct divine faculty of will. Evangelicals are not in agreement regarding this question. And, arguments for either position are not, in my view, overwhelmingly convincing although the unity of the divine nature, to me, suggests a oneness of will. But the second issue is whether "My own will" refers to Jesus' divine will or His human will. Yes, He came down from heaven as God, but then, after becoming flesh, perhaps then only as man He obeyed the Father.

But what is the evidence that in Christ there is a human faculty of will? It seems clearly taught in Luke 22:42, "Father, if it is Your will take this cup from Me; nevertheless not My will, but Yours be done." In the context, our Lord required strengthening by an angel and was "in agony." In my opinion, the divine faculty of will in Christ would not fear death, could not be in agony, and would not require strengthening by an angel. Only a human will would.

So, if Luke 22:42 is a sound reason to believe that Christ has a human will, in addition to a divine will as He also is God, then which will is the referent in John 6:38? Perhaps a clue is found in John 6:54 where flesh and blood are ascribed to Jesus. Of course, this would be unconvincing to Mormons as they believe that God is physical. But, John 1:14 instead teaches that the Son, who was not flesh before, became flesh in the incarnation.

As said elsewhere, in my opinion, the "flesh" (i.e., the nature of man) was added to the Person of the Son; the Son 's divine nature did not change. Perhaps John 6:54, then, should suggest to us that "will" in 6:36 refers to Jesus' human will. Adding credence to this interpretation is Philippians 2:8 where it is taught that it was in His human nature that Jesus became obedient: "And being found in the appearance of a man, He humbled Himself and became obedient" (that is, He was not before obedient).

John 14:28

> You have heard Me say to you, "I am going away and coming back to you." If you loved Me, you would rejoice because I said "I'm going to the Father," for My Father is greater than I.

If one interprets this verse to mean that the Father is greater than the Son as God, then, in what way is the Son as God to be considered inferior? Chapter four will take this question up again, and there specifics are given. But if the Father is eternal, almighty, omniscient, and immutable, and the Son is also all of these, then how is the Father greater? Please consider these questions in chapter four where it is argued that as the Persons in the Trinity have the same attributes, They, therefore, are the same. God.

1 Corinthians 11:3

> But I want you to know that the head of every
> man is Christ, the head of a woman is man, and
> the head of Christ is God.

It is likely that *kephalē* ("head") refers to authority over not the origin of.[40] If so, the verse is clearly stating that God is authority over Christ. But what is meant by "Christ"? Must the term have the deity of Christ as its referent? But Jesus who in these following references is called "Christ," specifically is said to have been born (Luke 2:11), have died (1 Peter 1:32), and have been resurrected (Acts 2:31). Such experiences must be only ascribed to Jesus' human nature. It likely then follows that 1 Corinthians 11:3 can mean that God is sovereign over the human nature of Christ not the divine nature. Of course, Mormons wrongly teach that Christ has only one nature.

1 Corinthians 15:28

> Now when all things are made subject to Him,
> then the Son Himself will also be subject to Him
> who put all things under Him, that God may be
> all in all.

But how can "Son" in 15:28 be understood as referring to the nature of God when 15:21 calls Christ "a man"? It is as "man" that the Son is subservient to the Father. He obeyed God as man. (Philippians 2:8).

Galatians 4:4,5

> But when the fullness of time had come, God
> sent forth His Son, born of a woman, born un-
> der the law to redeem those who were under
> the law, that we might receive the adoption of
> sons.

So, yes God the Father sent the Son. But the text stipulates that
it was the Son born of Mary, that is, it was Christ as man, who
was sent. Only as man could the Son die to redeem those under
the law. So, it is questionable that this verse teaches an eternal
relationship of one Person in God over Another. Nevertheless,
I have no issues with believing that in the economic, temporal
relationships of God to creation and also to salvation, God the
Father has the role of directing the activities of the Son and the
temporal activities of the Holy Spirit as well (e.g., John 14:16).

What I question is that the Father was, in eternity past, the
authority over the Son as God, since in my opinion, that would
only be likely possible for the Persons of God to be different in
being. Besides, in my view, as we read in Philippians 2:8 that
the Son "humbled Himself," (that is, He was not humbled by the
Father), I see grounds for believing that there was no personal
quality in the Son's divinity to be submissive. I think that in
ontological relationships, that is, God in Himself, the Persons
in God may relate in different ways than They do in their economic roles in time. Consider, for example, that in John 1:1 the
Son is identified as being God but there is no remark about the
Son being different in authority than God.

Philippians 2:6

> Who being in the form of God did not consider
> it robbery (Greek=*harpagmos*) to be (the) equal
> to God.

Okay, I have to be a little complex here. It has been argued that "form" in Philippians 2:6 refers to God's nature and "equal" refers to God's sovereignty, and that because there is an article (the) before the infinitive (to be) in the Greek, that functions as a wedge between nature and equality which has the force of separating the two. While the Son is in God's nature, He is not God's equal in authority is the claim. However, the force of the articular infinitive (the to be) here is much debated, and if the Greek *harpagmos* can be shown to indicate something that the Christ already possessed, then the meaning would be that the Son is both in God's nature and has God's authority.

And this is shown to be the case as Roy Hoover's Harvard Th.D. dissertation (reviewed in Harvard Theological Review, 56 (1971) 95-119) evidences by demonstrating when and how *harpagmos* is used idiomatically. The Son was God's equal, but chose not to use this equality to advance Himself is Hoover's conclusion. So, in Philippians 2:6 the Son in His deity (in God's nature) is equal in authority to the Father.

Hebrews 1:2

> Has in these last days spoken to us by His Son,
> whom He has appointed heir of all things,
> through whom He also made the worlds.

Since the Father created through the Son, it has been argued, this evidences that the Son is inferior in role than the Father. But must one deduce that from the divine activity in creation? Could it not with more understanding be opined that if the Father created through the Son that the Son has an equal role in creation? Were the Son of a lesser rank and the Father of a greater rank, then why is it even left a possibility that the Father relies on the Son to carry out the work of creation? Why would the Father need to create through the Son? Why not create without the Son? Could it be that the Father relies on the Son just as the Son does on the Father? Note that the very next verse informs that the Son upholds all things by His power. It is not even suggested there that the Son gets that power from the Father.

Hebrews 5:8

> Though He was a Son, yet He learned obedi-
> ence by the things He suffered.

Two items in this brief text make it clear that it was not the deity of the Son which is the referent. First, the Son learned, but as God the Son is omniscient. Second the Son suffered. But only as man can Christ suffer. Besides, the preceding verse alludes to the Son "in the days of His flesh." Therefore, Hebrews 5:8 cannot rightly be understood as convincing proof of the eternal role subordination of the Son.

The Son when incarnating was emptied of deity?

Millet[41] asserts that Paul teaches that Christ "emptied Himself of His Godhood that He might live and minister among mortals. Millet's reference is Philippians 2:6, where *heauton ekenōsen* can be translated as "emptied Himself." However, there are several reasons to reject this Mormon interpretation. First as shown above even Mormon Scriptures declare God to be changeless. Note also Moroni 8:18, "God is not a changeable Being" and Doctrines and Covenants 20:17, God is "the same unchangeable God."

Second, in verse 6 "being" in God's form is present tense. That is, even after the emptying, Christ continues to be in God's form. Third, the phrase "emptied Himself" has no object. It does not say that He emptied Himself of anything neither divinity nor the powers of divinity. Instead, what the apostle means by the emptying of Jesus is the adding of a human nature to the Person of our Lord, "taking the form of a bond servant" (2:7). His taking humanity was His emptying. But as God is changeless He did not divest Himself of deity.

The Son is the Only begotten in the flesh?

I am going to argue that Christ is the Father's only heavenly Son but not by a birthing. I think it likely that "Son of" denotes deity not origination (John 5:18). Christ is not one of many heavenly "spirit children." Part of my conjecture is based on the meaning of the Greek word often translated "only begotten." I will argue that the Greek *monogenēs* does not even mean a birthing, and that the adjective more likely refers to Christ's divinity not to His being born of Mary.

Christ is the unique Son of God because He is the only Son who is God! However, Ludlow's anthology in reference to John 3:16 avers that Christ is "the only begotten in the flesh" and His body was "the offspring of a mortal mother and an eternal Father."[42] `Yes, the adjective *monogenēs* which only John applies to Christ in five places (John 1:14, 18; 3:16, 18; and 1 John 4:9) is often rendered "only begotten" as it is in the NKJV. But other translations as the NEV translate the compound adjective with the meaning of "only," indicating "uniqueness," without the idea of a birthing. So, is John's point that Christ is the birthed Son or instead that He is the unique Son?

While we disagree over whether God the Father became husband to Mary and acted in that capacity with her (see chapter 1), both evangelicals and Mormons believe that Jesus is God's Son. So, what is there to argue about in regard to *monogenēs*? It is over whether John uses the adjective to indicate the Son's birthing from Mary. Mormons regularly insist that John's references (as in John 3:16) refer to Christ's being the only begotten of the Father in the flesh. [43]

But why would Mormons insist on that meaning? Could it be because they teach that the Father bore innumerable "spirit children" in heaven and that Christ is just one of these? Also, the Mormon teaching of exalted humans bearing innumerable "spirit children" becomes defunct were Christ, Himself, not the first born of the Father in heaven. So, being only begotten must refer, Mormons may reason, to His being born of Mary because we all, Christ too, are Christ's heavenly brethren born

65

of the Father in pre-mortality, they say. Mormons therefore reason, "only begotten" must refer to Jesus' mortal birth.

But are those five places where John applies monogenēs to Christ using the adjective to indicate that Christ was physically born or that He is unique due to His being the Father's only eternal Son and is God Himself? What is John's meaning? What's the difference, again? If the latter (uniqueness) is John's meaning, it opens up the idea that Christ is not just one of many "spirit children" of the Father. That, of course, would contradict the Mormon teaching of our pre-mortality.

We all know that John was a Jew, and we should know too that the first century church in the main used as their Bible the Old Testament translated into Greek (the Septuagint or LXX). And, the LXX uses monogenēs four times in the canonical Books and three times in the Apocryphal books. Let's look at these seven occasions. Let's ask whether their usage of the adjective shows that being born is meant (we all were physically born after all) or being unique? The translations are mostly those of Brenton.[44]

Judges 11:34 "She was his only (monogenēs) child; he had not another son or daughter." Clearly, the point here is that she was unique not that she was born.

Psalm 21:21 (22:20): "Deliver my soul from the sword my only begotten (monogenēs) from the power of the dog." The soul is not born however, so the meaning is that his soul is unique since the writer has only one.

Psalm 24:16. "I am an only (*monogenēs*) child and poor." Again, the idea is not being born but rather being alone.

Psalm 34:17: "Deliver my soul from their mischief, my only-begotten (*monogenēs*) one from the lions." He has only one soul so it is unique.

Tobit 3:17: "I am the only (*monogenēs*) (that is, in reference to a "daughter") of my father, neither has he any other child." The girl was unique having no siblings.

Tobit 8:17: "The only begotten (*monogeneis*) of their fathers." The children referenced were their fathers' only offspring.

Wisdom of Solomon 7:22: For in her (Wisdom) is an understanding spirit, holy, one only *monogenēs*." Wisdom is unique not born.

Let's also observe Luke's use of the adjective: In 7:12 the only son of his mother had died; In 8:42, the only daughter of a father was dying; in 9:28 also the father's son was an only child. Luke is not saying that these were born! So, why labor over John's meaning as suggested by Luke's and the Septuagint's usage? I do it to argue that the Son's being the only one of His kind did not begin when He became man. John is saying that Christ is unique not that He was born. In fact, there is reason to believe that John in 1:18 is saying that the Son is the *monogenēs* in His deity!

Let's be reminded that Mormons are not opposed to modifying the King James Bible to justify their doctrines. So, when

Joe Smith produced his "Inspired Translation" he completely omitted Mark 13:32[45] probably because that verse suggested that the omniscient, one-natured Christ of Mormonism was ignorant of somethings. Mormons disavow that Christ has two intellects one divine and one human. But while there is no evidence suggesting that Mark 13:32 is not original, there is strong evidence that John 1:18 is not originally as the NKJV represents it, i.e., "The only begotten Son."

It more likely originally read, "The only God." (See The New English Translation for example) Christ is the unique God as He is one in essence with the Father and the Spirit. The two earliest copies of John we have (Papyrus 66 and Papyrus P75) say "*monogenēs* (that is, in my opinion, the unique) God."[46] And there is no apparent reason to suggest why a scribe would change "Son" to "God" given that elsewhere in John the adjective describes "Son." So, Christ is God's unique Son in His eternality not in His humanity with the effect that He was not the "first born," child in heaven as Mormons teach. He is, instead, the only child (i.e.,"Son") of heaven, and, yes, of course, in His Incarnation, He still continues as God's Son. Neither His Person nor His past can change. John, in my opinion calls Christ *monogenēs* to indicate our Lord's unique relationship to God not to inform us that He was born.

The Son had to work out His own salvation?

I find the Mormon McConkie's position to be both biblically untenable and offensive to the majesty of Christ. McConkie feels so strongly about his teaching that he must repeat it. He first states, "Christ, Himself, first worked out His own salvation,"[47] and later he elaborates a bit saying, (Christ) also had to work out His own salvation, to serve in mortality, to humble Himself before the Father, to keep the commandments, to endure to the end.[48] Did our Lord Jesus humble Himself and keep God's commandments? Yes. But did He do these things to save Himself? No. Observe the reason given in Hebrews 5:8, 9,

> Though He was a Son, yet He learned obedience by the things He suffered. And having been perfected, He became the author of eternal salvation to all who obey Him.

Christ did not become perfect in order to save Himself for He, Himself, needed no redemption. Christ asked the Father to forgive others but never asked for forgiveness for Himself. Christ knew no sin (2 Corinthians 5:21). He was tempted, but never sinned as a result (Hebrews 4:15). And, in fact, He never committed any sin (1 Peter 2:22). Yes, it is offensive to the biblical portrayal of the perfection of our Lord Jesus for Mormons to teach that Christ needed to work out His own salvation.

The Son did know the time of His return?

The Mormon disregard for the teaching of the Bible is clearly evidenced in the manner in which they subordinate the Bible's teaching to their preconceived doctrines. Since Mormons deny that Christ exists in both a divine and a human nature (since God and man are the same race), and a nature would include intelligence, Mormons wish to erase the teaching about Christ in Mark 13:32,

> But of that day and hour (i.e., the time of His second coming) no one knows, not even the angels in heaven, nor the Son, but only the Father.

McConkie explains, "These words are deleted from the Inspired Version; Jesus, of course, since He knows all things, knows the exact time of His return." And, what is that tenet to be erased so as not to conflict with Mormon "erudition"? It is that in His humanity Christ does not know some things (Mark 13:32) but in His deity, He knows everything (John 16:30; 21:17). That is because Christ exists in two natures each having its own intelligence. So, where a Bible verse teaches a doctrine which contradicts Mormon theology, Mormons just remove that offensive verse!

The Son has wives?

We should remind ourselves of the Mormon doctrine of exaltation. It refers to living evermore in heavenly family units as husbands and wives and bearing children. [49] But wait. The resurrected Christ also experiences exaltation because He is a saved being. [50] How then can Christ now exalted live in such a family unit without having a wife or wives to bear His heavenly offspring? The Mormon Orson Pratt, who was designated to teach the doctrines of the Mormon religion by Joe, himself, comes to rescue us from this dilemma. Pratt reasons that Jesus must bear His own heavenly brood just as His Father does. So, Pratt suggests that as Jesus is said to love certain holy women (John 11:5), ergo, they likely were His wives who will bear Christ's spirit children after they are resurrected. (So, would that make Christ their daddy and God the Father their grand daddy?)

Pratt refers his readers to Psalm 45:8,9 saying that this text proves that Jesus is husband to individual women.[51] But the women Christ loved—in my opinion not in a sexual way-- were neither daughters of kings nor was one of then a "queen"! So clearly, the text is not meant to be taken literally. It is rather that many nations (i.e., "kings daughters) will have individuals converted to our Lord and that the "queen" in Psalm 45 is the Church which is Jesus' only bride (John 3: 29; Ephesians 5:23-26). Nor do the Gospels ever say that Jesus ever married a woman. Again, Mormons fabricate doctrines not in the New Testament and then claim to be restoring the Gospel by doing that.

The Son after death was exalted receiving again the deity which He had given up?

Mormons teach that after Christ gave up His divinity and the powers thereof when incarnating, He "went from grace to grace" until He eventually after the resurrection "gained the fulness of all things; and all power was given to Him in heaven and on earth." [52] A difficulty with this interpretation is that in His earthly existence He is said to remain in the nature of God. "Being" in Philippians 2:6 is in the present tense (huparchōn). The customary and ongoing Greek present tense indicates "an ongoing state," and the gnomic present means much the same [53] Therefore, Christ never relinquished His deity or powers when becoming man. Furthermore, even after His Incarnation and before His resurrection, Christ remained God (John 20:28).

Review Questions Chapter 2

1. What in the Gospels shows that Christ was not emptied of deity when incarnating?

2. How are Christ's two natures demonstrated in the Gospels?

3. What do the earliest Greek copies of John 1:18 inform us about the Greek *monogenēs*?

4. How does Philippians 2 teach that Christ never was emptied of deity?

5. Why would Mormons insist that Christ being "only begotten" refers to His body born of Mary?

6. What in the New Testament shows that Christ did not need personal redemption?

7. What in the New Testament tells us that Christ did not marry individual women?

8. What did Hoover's ThD. dissertation show?

9. How might Judges 11:34 contradict Mormon doctrine?

10. What are some issues in John 6:38?

End Notes Chapter 2

1. Stephan E. Robinson. *Are Mormons Christians?* (Salt Lake: Bookcraft, 1991), 72, 73.

2. Philip Schaff (ed.) The Creeds of Christendom, vol 1. (Grand Rapids: Baker, 1998), 58, 60.

3. Athenagoras. *A Plea for the Christians.* X.

4. *Ibid,*

5. XI

6. Tertullian. *On Prescription Against Heretics.* XIII, XL; *Against Marcion* III.

7. *Against Marcion* VII.

8. XVI

9. *Ad Nationes* IV.

10. *Against Praxeas,* II.

11. IV, XXV; *Apology,* XXI.

12. *Praxeas,* XXVII.

13. Origen. *De Principiis,* Preface.

14. I.III.3.; II.IV.4.

15. I.I.2.

16. I.I.8.

17. I.II.5-7.

18. I.II.12.

19. II.VI.1.

20. I.I.8.

21. I.III.1; II.VI.3.

22. Robinson, 86.

23. Richard R. Hopkins. *Biblical Mormonism.* (Bountiful, Utah: Horizons, 1994), 63,64.

24. 34.

25. D.A. Carson. *Exegetical Fallacies.* (Grand Rapids: Baker, 1984), 26-29.

26. William F. Arndt and F. Wilber Gingrich. *A Greek-English Lexicon of the New Testament.* (Chicago: University Press),1957), 734.

27. Wilhelm Michaelis. *Prōtotokos in Theological Dictionary of the New Testament, 6.* Gerhard Kittel (ed.). (Grand Rapids: Eerdmans, 1968), 878.

28. Karl Heinz Bartels. *Monogenēs* in the *New International Dictionary of New Testament Theology, 2.* Colin Brown, ed. (Grand Rapids: Regency, 1986),668.

29. Shaff, vol III, 393.

30. 608.

31. 850.

32. 814.

33. Hopkins, 103.

34. Bruce R. McConkie. *Mormon Doctrine.* (Salt Lake, *1979*) *589;* Robert L. Millet, ed.. *LDS Beliefs.* (Salt Lake: Deseret, 2011), 562.35. Daniel H. Ludlow, ed. *Jesus Christ and His Gospel.* (Salt Lake: Deseret, 1992) 15.

36. Robert L. Millet. *A Different Jesus?* (Grand Rapids: Eerdmans, 2005),73.

37. McConkie, *Doctrine, 129.*

38. David J. Ridges. *Mormon Beliefs and Doctrines Made Easier.* (Springville, Utah, CFI, 2007), 119.

39. Millet, *Beliefs, 263.*

40. Wayne Grudem. "Does *Kephale (Head) Mean Source of or Authority Over in Greek Literature?*" Trinity Journal, 6, NS,1985.

41. Millet. *Claiming Christ.* (Grand Rapids: Brazos, 2007), 79.

42. Ludlow, 264.

43. McConkie, *Doctrine, 546.*

44. Sir Lancelot C.L. Brenton. *The Septuagint with Apocrypha: Greek and English.* (Peabody, Mass:1998).

45. *Joseph Smith's New Translation of the Bible* (Independence, Mo.: Herald House, 1970).

46. Bruce M. Metzger. *A Textual Commentary of the Greek New Testament.* (Germany: UBS, 2007), 169.

47. McConkie. *Doctrinal New Testament Commentary, vol II.* (Salt Lake: Bookcraft, 1971),496.

48. 533.

49.Ridges 92; Ludlow 159.

50. McConkie, Doctrine 257.

52. Orson Pratt. *The Seer.* (U.S.A.: Eborn Books, 2009), 159.

52. McConkie, Doctrine, 129; Millett, *A Different Jesus, 67.*

53. Daniel B. Wallace. *Greek Grammar Beyond the Basics. (Grand Rapids: Zondervan, 1996), 521, 523.*

3

GOD THE HOLY SPIRIT

Joseph Smith once bloviated that he knew more "than all the world put together" because he had the Holy Spirit in him. Others preaching salvation, he said, are "unlearned in the things of God and have not the gift of the Holy Ghost."[1] Yet it will require a great deal of imaginative apologetics to align LDS teaching about the Holy Spirit with the doctrine of the Bible. I will comment on two issues.

The Holy Spirit is the Father's "spirit child"?

First, Mormons assert that the Holy Spirit is the "spirit son" of the Father. [2] It will be remembered that Mormons believe that we all (and the Holy Spirit is one of the "all") were begotten as "spirit children" and lived in heaven with God.[3] These spirit children were not equal in intelligence or faithfulness and some were wicked in their pre-mortality. Jesus Christ was the first born of these spirit children,[4] and the Holy Spirit would have been perhaps the second according to Mormon thought? So, the Holy Spirit had a beginning.

Or, did He? Hebrews 9:14 informs that the Holy Spirit is eternal. Yes, I know Mormons teach that we all existed as eternal intelligences. But the verse does not say that the Spirit eternally existed merely as an intelligence. Hebrews 9:14 states that the Spirit, Himself, is eternal. How could that have been made clearer? Nor, does the Bible anywhere state that anyone else existed eternally as an "intelligence." It should be expected that Mormons respond to Hebrews 9:14 without allusions to doctrines not found in the Bible to explain away their faulty exegesis.

The Holy Spirit is spatial and is in the form of a man?

Another LDS error is their teaching that the Holy Spirit is spatially limited and is in the form of a man. The Mormon study guide of LDS doctrine *Gospel Principles* [5] explains:

> The Holy Ghost... is a spirit that has the form and likeness of a man. He can only be in one place at a time, but His influence can be everywhere at the same time.

But do biblical texts which allude to the Holy Spirit suggest that He is in human form, that His Person is limited to being in one place at a time, and therefore that only His influence can be everywhere? In no particular order I list 20 Bible references below which are not in harmony with these Mormon claims. There will be some repetition of ideation in these Scriptures. Many more verses easily could have been be included.

(1) The Holy Spirit fell on all those who heard the Word. (Acts 10:44)

There appears to have been a number of people who heard Peter speak that day as Cornelius had assembled "relatives and close friends." (Acts 10:24) Observe that the text states that it is the Spirit Himself, not His influence, which is the subject of the action. He, Himself, simultaneously fell on all of them. There is no suggestion either in the passage that the Spirit fell on those present one at a time. We can also note that whatever is the meaning of the Spirit "falling on," it doesn't fit well with the concept of a spatially limited One who is in the form of a man. How does One in human form "fall" on a number of individuals? He cannot, so Acts 10:44 does not support the Mormon doctrine.

(2) Be filled with the Spirit. (Ephesians 5:18)

So, if the concept of the Holy Spirit being in the form of a spatially limited man is held, how can the Spirit "fill" multitudes of believers at the same time? It will not do to say, "Oh, this means the Spirit's influence not His Person." For only a few verses away, the apostle speaks of grieving the Spirit (4:30). But, how does one grieve an influence? And, how does One in human form fill others in who are also in human form? He cannot. So Ephesians 5:18 does not support the Mormon doctrine.

(3). "The Spirit of the LORD will carry you to a place." (1 Kings 18:12)

Are we to imagine that the Holy Spirit having the arms, as one in human form would have, lifted Elijah and, having legs in human form as well, very hurriedly ran Elijah about? The Mormon understanding of the Holy Spirit which must adapt to God being a big man becomes tediously ridiculous in view of Scriptures as 1 Kings 18:12. The meaning must be more like the idea that the Holy Spirit used His miraculous abilities to transport Elijah to a place; the activity in the text does not endorse the notion that the Spirit is in the form of a man. Where does the Bible ever say that the Holy Spirit has arms and legs? It does not, so 1 Kings 18:12 does not support Mormon doctrine.

(4). The Spirit of God dwells in you. (1 Corinthians 3:16).

It does not say "The influence of the Spirit dwells in you"! Texts as this are obviously in contradiction to the LDS teaching that the Holy Spirit cannot be everywhere. For how could He not be everywhere if He dwells in believers who themselves are everywhere? We might do well to note that the Holy Spirit is called a Helper, a *paraklētos*, in John 14:16. This noun means "one called in to support."[6] It does not mean an influence is "called in to support." Yet, if the Holy Spirit is the One actively supporting Christians universally, then how can the Spirit be limited to one place? He cannot, so 1 Corinthians 3:18 does not support the Mormon doctrine.

(5.) We have all been made to drink into one Spirit." (1 Corinthians 12:13)

The likely meaning is that believers have received the Spirit by the very real experience of Spirit baptism (perhaps cross references are John 1:33 and Acts 1:5?) and thus are united in one body. Evangelicals disagree on what "Spirit baptism" is. Some say it is a "second blessing" with speaking in tongues as the evidence of that experience, yet, others do not believe that. But the point now is why would Paul even figuratively allude to innumerable believers drinking the Spirit were the Spirit localized? Were Paul wishing to teach that the Holy Spirit is in the form of a man, why would the apostle speak of drinking Him? He would not, so 1 Corinthians 12:13 does not support the Mormon doctrine.

(6). Led by the Spirit. (Romans 8:14).

Being sons of God means being led by the Spirit of God. It does not say being led "by the influence of God's Spirit"! So, this verse also evidences that the Holy Spirit cannot be confined to one location since those being led do not reside in one location. The LDS insistence on the humanness of God is dashed to pieces by the biblical teaching of the omnipresence of God. How could the Spirit be confined to one locality if He, Himself, is leading believers all over the world? He could not, so Romans 8:14 does not support the Mormon doctrine.

(7.) "He has filled him with the Spirit of God." Exodus 35:31

Bezalel was filled with the Holy Spirit enabling him to create artistic works in metal, jewels, and wood. Again, it is not said that it was the Spirit's influence that filled this craftsman but the Holy Spirit, Himself, filled Bezalel. Spirit filling before the ascension of our Lord Jesus appears to have been limited to chosen individuals. However, this cannot be rightly deemed merely to be the influence of the Spirit, as it should be noted again that the use of the Hebrew word for the verb "fill" (*mala*) indicates that the thing itself is filling not the influence of a thing: "fill their sacks with grain." (Genesis 42:25) The meaning is not fill the sacks with the influence of the grain. "I will fill this temple with glory." (Haggai 2:7). It is the glory itself which will fill the temple! Likewise, the Holy Spirit, Himself, filled Bezalel. Therefore, the Holy Spirit cannot be "in human form" so, Exodus 35:31 does not support Mormon doctrine.

(8.) "Did you receive the Spirit by the works of the law or by the hearing of faith." (Galatians 3:2)

The Mormon doctrinal book edited by Ludlow includes the remark "The Holy Ghost will not dwell in the heart of an unrighteous person...Should the individual thereafter cease to be clean and obedient, the Holy Ghost will withdraw." It is true that the contributor in Ludlow's book stipulates that the Holy Spirit only dwells in one's heart "in a figurative sense."[7] Why does Ludlow qualify the Holy Spirit's indwelling as "figurative"? It obviously is because the Holy Spirit in Mormon theology is a Man. A Man cannot indwell another man. But how does an "influence" withdraw? And, were the apostle not wishing to indicate that the Spirit, Himself, is received, not merely His power, then why didn't Paul make that clear? Why did Paul not ask, "Did you receive the influence or power of the Spirit?" But, he does not, so Galatians 3:2 does not support the Mormon doctrine.

(9.) "Where the Spirit of the Lord is there is liberty." (2 Corinthians 3:17)

And, where is the Spirit of the Lord? He is with the Corinthians. But is He not also with the Galatians, and the Romans, and the Thessalonians? Yet Paul does not say that anything less than the presence of the Holy Spirit is his meaning. But despite this unreserved attestation to the universal presence of the Spirit, the Mormons have invented a doctrine to refute the Pauline teaching of the omnipresence of the Spirit. It is called, "The Light of Christ." It is defined as "a power and influence that proceeds forth from the presence of God to fill the immensity of space....It is in this way that the Holy Ghost makes His influence felt."[8] But the reader will note that Paul is not saying that it is the Spirit's power or influence only which is everywhere. Paul says it is the Spirit of the Lord Himself. So, 2 Corinthians 3:17 does not support the Mormon doctrine.

(10). "And they were all filled with the Holy Spirit." (Acts 2:4).

Observe again that Luke does not say they were filled with "the power or influence of the Holy Spirit." The New Testament remarks on having God's power as in 2 Corinthians 6:7, "by the power of God" (see also 2 Timothy 1:8; 1 Peter 1:5). One should not think that God is identical to His power. His power is a quality but God is the Person. The power of the Spirit is alluded to in Romans 15:13. And, Romans 15:19 reads, "in mighty signs and wonders by the power of the Spirit of God." Likewise note Acts 10:38, "God anointed Jesus of Nazareth with the Holy Spirit and with power." In these texts, the Spirit Himself is clearly differentiated from His power or influence! Consequentially, when the Holy Spirit is distinctly referenced without mentioning His power, the allusion should be understood as meaning the Person of the Spirit Himself not merely to His influence. Therefore, Acts 2:4 does not support the Mormon doctrine.

(11). "Go therefore and make disciples of all the nations...The Spirit of Truth...will testify of Me." (Matthew 28:19; John 15:26).

The Holy Spirit will testify of Jesus in all the nations! So, how is the Spirit confined to one locality at a time? Does He rush from one place to another place with incredible rapidity? This, exactly, is the teaching of the Mormon Hopkins.[9] God can "travel to any spot instantaneously." Just picture that! God moving all over the earth in an instant. So, does hearing the testifying take place instantly as well? Are the ears of millions miraculously changed to receive and comprehend communication from God about Jesus in a split second thus enabling the Spirit to move on in His journey from one place to the next place of testifying? But wait a minute. Observe that Peter's message in Acts 2:14-40 was not given in an instant and note that the message given was by the Holy Spirit coming on him (1:8). The Holy Spirit is doing the testimony, but it is not done instantly. How could it be when the testimony must be heard which requires time? This is why John 15:26 does not support the Mormon doctrine.

(12). "The Spirit bears witness with our spirit." (Romans 8:16).

Again, it is the Person of the Holy Spirit which is said to be witnessing to our spirits not merely His influence. However, as we individuals (and our spirits dwelling within us) are widely dispersed all over the world, it is only by the Spirit's omnipresence that this witnessing can occur. Consequently, Romans 8:16 does not support the Mormon doctrine.

(13). "When He, the Spirit of truth, has come, He will guide you into all truth." (John 16:13).

The reader will note that this verse references the Holy Spirit by a masculine pronoun (*ekeinos*). Therefore, it is not the influence of the Spirit which will guide the apostles; it is the Himself who will do that. But this would seemingly require the Spirit to not be confined to one location at a time as the apostles were not restricted to one place. A spatially limited Spirit could not fulfill the promise of Jesus Christ, and so John 16:13 does not support the Mormon doctrine.

(14). "No one can say 'Jesus is Lord' but by the Holy Spirit." (1 Corinthians 12:3)

So, on any given Sunday in multiple localities believers are confessing Jesus Christ as Lord. But they are not confessing this except by the Holy Spirit. It does not say it is by merely the Spirit's influence but by the Spirit Himself. But what in the context indicates that Paul has the Spirit Himself in mind and not the Spirit's power? Observe that in just a few verses away, the apostle writes that the Spirit gives gifts as "He wills." An influence does not give gifts. A power does not have a will. And, an influence or power is not a "He." That is why 1 Corinthians 12:3 does not support the Mormon doctrine.

(15). "God has sent forth the Spirit of His Son into your hearts." (Galatians 4:6).

The universal presence of the Holy Spirit is clearly shown by this text. For how could the Spirit not be everywhere at the same time if He resides in the heart of every believer? In their insistence that He is spatially confined and in the form of a man, the Mormons would rob us of the full blessing of salvation by depriving of us the actual indwelling of the Spirit of God. Galatians 4:6 does not support Mormon doctrine.

(16). "Did you receive the Holy Spirit when you believed?" (Acts 19:2)

The notion that it is receiving the Spirit's influence and not His Person which was in Paul's question is shown to be incorrect given the context. After being baptized in Christ's name the Holy Spirit "came upon them." How does an influence come on anything? The activity of the Person of the Holy Spirit often indicates that it is His Person not His influence which is the subject. Note, for example Isaiah 63:10: "They grieved His Holy Spirit." How does one grieve an influence? Acts 19:2 does not support Mormon doctrine.

(17). "The one and the same Spirit works all these things." (1 Corinthians 12:11)

In this verse we learn that the Holy Spirit provides charismata to believers in Christ's "body" (i.e., the church) according to His (the Spirit's) will. But, an influence, again, does not have a will. However, the believers who comprise the Church are in many locations. They are all over the world. Should we imagine that the Spirit hurries around to every location wherein believers reside to distribute His gifts? But why could He not from His heavenly abode do this? It is because the context stipulates that believers are baptized by the Spirit. If the Spirit resides only in one place, then how can He baptize believers in many places? 1 Corinthians 12:11 does not support Mormon doctrine.

(18). "Made alive by the Spirit." (1 Peter 3:18)

Again, it can be noted by texts as Luke 4:14, "Jesus returned in the power of the Spirit," that the biblical writers differentiate between the Spirit's power and the Spirit Himself. So, when a text has as its named exclusive subject "the Spirit," without reference to the Spirit's influence or power, one should take this as a referent to the Holy Spirit Himself. But as those who are being "made alive" are scattered about in many different locations, it follows that the Spirit, Himself, is not confined to one locality at a time. 1 Peter 3:18 does not support Mormon doctrine.

(19). "The Spirit of Christ who was in them was indicating when He testified before hand the sufferings of Christ." 1 Peter 1:11

The Holy Spirit was in the Old Testament prophets (1:10) who prophesied of Christ. But how could He be "in them" if He is in the form of a man? That which is in the form of a person cannot indwell many other persons. So, 1 Peter 1:11 does not support Mormon doctrine.

(20). "I will pour out my Spirit on all flesh." Acts 2:17

But if the Holy Spirit is not universally present, then how can He be poured out on "all flesh"? If He is in the form of a Man, how is He "poured out" at all? The LDS teaching on the Person of the Holy Spirit falters in view of what the Bible proclaims about Him. Acts 2:17 does not support Mormon doctrine.

Review Questions Chapter 3

1. Define the Mormon teaching about the Person of the Spirit.

2. How do Genesis 42:25 and Haggai 2:7 conflict with Mormon doctrine?

3. Where and how does the Bible distinguish between the Person of the Spirit and the power of the Spirit?

4. What did Joe Smith say about himself that could be interpreted as a severe case of self- obsession?

5. What Mormon teaching does Hebrews 9:14 contradict and why?

6. What do Mormons mean by "The Light of Christ"?

7. What are two views among evangelicals on "Spirit baptism"?

8. What Mormon teaching about the Spirit does 1 Kings 18:12 appear to refute?

9. How do believers confessing Jesus as Lord indicate that the Spirit is not confined to one place at a time?

10. How does the Spirit being called a *paraklētos* contradict Mormon teaching?

End notes chapter 3

1. King Follet Discourse.

2. Daniel H. Ludlow (ed). *Jesus Christ and His Gospel.* (Salt Lake: Deseret, 1992), 231.

3. Richard R. Hopkins. *Biblical Mormonism.* (Bountiful, Utah: Horizon, 1994), 101.

4. David J. Ridges. *Mormon Beliefs and Doctrines Made Easier.* (Springville, Utah: CFI,2007), 106.

5. *Gospel Principles.* (Salt Lake: Church of Jesus Christ of Latter-Day Saints, 1997), 37.

6. James Hope Moulton and George Milligan. *The Vocabulary of the Greek New Testament.* (London: Hodder and Stoughton, 1952), 485.

7. Ludlow, 231, 232.

8. Robert L. Millet. *LDS Beliefs.* (Salt Lake: Deseret, 2011), 393.

9. Hopkins, 58.

4

GOD'S UNITY AND TRINITY

Some definitions: By "being" and "essence" I refer to the same thing, namely the nature of God. By "Being" with a capital I refer to the one God, Himself. By "Persons" I refer to the three Members in the one Being.

True God has the qualities of God

Let's review some of the qualities or attributes of God according to the Bible. First, God is everywhere. "Heaven and the heaven of heavens cannot contain You/ Do I not fill heaven and earth? says the LORD?" (1 Kings 8:27; Jeremiah 23:23). What other Being besides God in the Bible is said to be omnipresent? There is none! Second, God also knows everything. "I am God and there is none liked Me, Declaring the end from the beginning/ Known to God from eternity are all His works." (Isaiah 46:9, 10; Acts 15:18). What other Being besides God in the Bible is said to be omniscient? There is none! Third, God has all power. "I am God almighty/ Is anything too hard for Jehovah?" (Genesis 17:1/ 18:14). What other Being in the Bible is said to be omnipotent? There is none!

I believe that if an entity does not have these attributes which God has, then that one is not really God. Yes, I know that Mormons imagine that deceased, exalted humans have the same powers of God "in heaven and on earth."[1] But, what is their Scriptural proof of that? I have seen no biblical evidence offered in Mormon literature which shows that men become all powerful. And, let the Mormons try to prove from the Bible that what are sometimes called "gods" remotely resemble the One who is omnipresent, omniscient, and omnipotent. Yes, some in the Bible are called "gods" but these have limited authority or power under God over other individuals or instead are false, non-existent, pagan deities. Mormons wish to make you believe that such as these are really Gods. Mormons assert that in order to attempt to convince you that the Mormon tenets of a plurality of deities and men becoming Gods are biblical truths. Don't believe it. They are not biblical truths!

Evangelical opinions about God

Evangelicals, in contrast, believe that there is only one God but that there are three eternal and equal, distinct members in the one God whom we call "Persons." These "Persons" are not separate Beings but comprise only one Being which together we call a "Trinity." Are three "Persons" existing in one Being unlike what we observe in all other living things including man? Of course, but we believe that a triune God is what Scripture teaches, and evangelicals don't see it as biblical to create God in man's image. And, note that according to Ephesians 4:24 and Colossians 3:10 man existing in God's image consists of being righteous, holy, and knowledgeable, not in being like

God in the powers or components of His Being. So, we are not required to say that since a human being is not three in one, therefore God cannot be a Trinity in the sense that evangelicals teach Him to be.

Evangelicals are committed to the belief in God's triune Being because the Bible while naming three who are God speaks of there being only one God: "Hear, O Israel: the LORD our God, the LORD is one." (Deuteronomy 6:4) Yes, I know that Mormons have countered that this text means that Jehovah (the Son) is only one God among the Gods and *Elohim* is another, but it cannot be intelligently argued that *Jehovah* is a different Being than *Elohim* as shown in both chapter two and below.

Yet, it clearly is also taught in Scripture that the three Members in God interact with each other. So, for want of a better term, we call them "Persons." We see each of the "Persons" as an eternal and equal subsistence in God who has the entirety of the divine nature of God. The Father's nature is identical to, not greater, than that of the Son and the Spirit. Rather, the Three are equal in being. God cannot be greater than God because that which is less than God in essence and/or attributes is not God.

The Father and the Son

It is true that some of the ways the Persons in God function in interacting with the creation indicate that the Father in some instances has an executive sort of position in how God temporally relates to the world. But this is not a difference in essence but a difference in role. How the Persons relate to the universe is not necessarily indicative of how the Persons relate to each other within God. The Father, for example, economically sent the self-humbled One ("he humbled Himself"-Philippians 2:8) into the world (Galatians 4:4), but the Son of God ontologically is glorious (John 1:14), is in the Father's bosom (John1:18), and shares in the Father's glory just as John 17:5 reads,

> And now, O Father, glorify Me together with Yourself, with the glory which I had with you before the world was.

I should comment on John 17:5 though it is a bit technical. "With you" is a good translation of the Greek (*para soi*). While the preposition (para) when used with a genitive substantive can mean "from" here it is used with the dative pronoun (*soi*) and so indicates only a nearness.[2] Therefore, it is incorrect to interpret John 17:5 as meaning that in His pre-incarnate state the Son's glory was given Him by the Father. Eternally He shared the same glory with the Father; the Father did not provide the Son's deity with glory. Yet in His humanity, the Son is glorified (Philippians 2:9) by the Father. So, accordingly, I argue that temporal activities among the Persons in the Trinity do not necessarily reflect eternal relationships.

Mormon arguments for the plurality of God

Mormons, of course, deny that there is only one God. Brigham Young, for example, declared, "How many Gods there are I do not know." To give credence to such an exclamation -- which obviously contradicts the shema in Deuteronomy 6:4 -- the Mormon apologists work hard to argue for a plurality of Gods. I will respond below to ten of their arguments.

1. Mormons may say the baptism of Jesus in Matthew 3:16, 17 shows that there are at least three separate Gods.

> When He had been baptized, Jesus came up immediately from the water; and behold the heavens were open to Him, and He saw the Spirit of God descending like a dove and alighting on Him. And suddenly a voice came from heaven saying, "This is My beloved Son in whom I am well pleased."

I will first respond by noting that Christ's humanity, that which was born and died, was baptized not His deity. I don't believe that God who fills heaven and earth (Ephesians 4:10) or is with believers everywhere (Matthew 28:20) can be covered by water. Therefore, it should not be argued that Jesus' baptism is evidence that the Son and the Father are separate Beings. His humanity is different from His deity. In one nature He wearies at Jacob's well (John 4:6). In the other He upholds the universe (Colossians 1:17). I then will contend that the Mormon position is in error because The Spirit and the Father are one Being as God's activities of indwelling believers and creating the universe demonstrate.

So, Mormons say that since we see the Son being baptized, the Spirit descending, and the Father speaking from heaven the Three must be different Gods. But, as said, I instead see it that the nature of the One who was baptized in His humanity is different in nature from the Father, but He in His divinity is the same in essence as the Father. It was He who in a human nature in the flesh grew in size and knowledge (Luke 2:52), that was tempted by the devil, and later suffered under the whip and expired on the cross which was baptized. One cannot kill God!

Such conditions and experiences cannot be applicable to the almighty (Revelation 1:8) and unchangeable (Hebrews 1:11, 12) Son of God. It was not God the Son as He exists in His divinity which was being baptized, but it was instead the Son in the human nature which He added to His eternal Person by "Taking the form of a bond servant and coming in the likeness of men" (Philippians 2:7).

This One being baptized, therefore, was not God as God is but was Christ who "had to be made"-- and therefore, He was not before—"like His brethren." (Hebrews 2:17). That, by the way, evidences that God is not a man since Jesus was not a man before His incarnation. That the divine nature of the One being baptized cannot be localized, which was required in the baptismal experience, is proven by His filling the universe (Ephesians 4:10) and residing within believers all over the world (Colossians 1:27). How could He who in His deity is everywhere be covered with water? That which is baptized is only His humanity.

It will not do, therefore, to argue that Christ in His baptism must be equivalent to Christ in His nature as God. Therefore, the argument that Matthew 3:16, 17 evidences there being three Gods is mistaken because Christ in His deity is not confined to the body which was baptized. The essence of God the Son is not proven as being different from the essence of the Father because it was only Christ in His humanity that was baptized. In His deity, Christ is the same God as the Father. But, there remains the issue of whether The Father and the Holy Spirit are the same God.

We might note that in Matthew 3:16, 17 God the Holy Spirit being manifested spatially in the appearance of a dove need not be evidence either that the Spirit is a different Being than God the Father. One reads in 1 Corinthians 3:17 that believers are the temples of God (not of Gods). I take "God" here to refer to the Father as in chapter 3 this appears to be Paul's meaning (e.g., 3:23). So, how does God the Father dwell in believers? Well, as 3:16 states, it is by "the Spirit of God (who) dwells in you." In other words, the Father dwelling in believers is synonymous with the Spirit dwelling in believers. That demonstrates that the Father and the Spirit, while different "Persons" (given their interactions as in John 14:16 and Acts 2:7) are one and the same Being. They are one God.

Therefore, that God's voice came from heaven does not require that the Father is different in being from He who is descending like a dove. In Psalm 104, for example, God *Elohim* whom

Mormons say is the Father and *Jehovah* whom Mormons say is the Son are both named as being involved in creation. But so is the Holy Spirit (Psalm104:30); He also creates. These three are each involved in doing the same thing. But only one God created. In other words, the Three are the same divine Being.

That only one God created is proven by texts as Revelation 10:6:

> And swore by Him (note: **not by Them**) who lives for ever and ever, who created heaven and all the things that are in it, the earth and the things that are in it, and the sea and the things that are in it.

Please note that the verb translated "created" (that is *ktizō* in its present tense) in the original Greek is singular in number which demonstrates that only one Being is the subject of that verb not three! Yet, the Father, the Son, and the Spirit each created. Three in One! Thus, the unity of God is clearly evidenced despite there being three "Persons" involved in the creation! The three "Persons" are one and the same God. Why are Mormons teaching that Persons in the Godhead are different Gods? It better correlates to their heresy that we may become Gods too. Recall Joe's admonition "You have got to learn to be Gods yourselves." (King Follet Discourse)

2. Mormons may say that as Christ was incarnated, that demonstrates His not being in the same essence as the Father.

And the Word became flesh and dwelt among
us, and we beheld His glory, as of the only begotten of the Father, full of grace and truth.
(John 1:14)

Mormons argue that as the Son is said to incarnate but the
Father did not, that shows that the Two cannot be one in essence. What Mormons cannot concede is that our Lord's becoming human was not a changing of His divine nature but
adding humanity to His Person. In His divinity the Son remains a Person in the one God.

 Christ's Person includes the unchangeable divine nature +
the added human nature. This subject is thoroughly covered
in chapter 2, but in brief review we should remind ourselves
again of Paul's teaching in Philippians 2:6, 7: (1) The Son exists
in God's nature (note: not natures; there is only one nature in
God.) As there is only one divine nature, there is only one God.
Form" refers to nature. In verse 6 the verb "being" (that is "existing") is present tense, so the Son never gave up that divine
nature. He remains fully God even though He became human
as well. (2) Then, verses 7 and 8 tell us that the Son who eternally and immutably (Hebrews 1:12) exists in God's nature also
took the nature of a bondservant which is human. One nature
plus one nature equals two natures. In His first and almighty
nature He remains one in essence or being with the Father,
but in His second, He has a limited human nature . That was
required because only as man could He could die for our sins.
As God He could not. Mormons, who just don't get it, make a

huge theological mistake in their denial of the two natures in Christ.

3. Mormons may say *Elohim* and *Jehovah* (that is, "*Yahweh*") are two different Gods.

If Mormons can convincingly support this, then belief in there only one divine Being is shown to be compromised. But in my view the Old Testament clearly teaches that the two are the same God. Recall that in the King James translation *Elohim* is rendered "God" and *Jehovah* is LORD. ("Lord" with only the first letter capitalized would be *Adonay*). But, the names *Elohim* and *Jehovah* appear together over and over again in ways which can only be understood as the two referencing the same God. Here are a few examples which show that the two are one:

(1).Genesis 2:4: "The LORD God made the earth." But as Revelation 10:6 demonstrates, only one God created. Note also Malachi 2:10: "Has not one God created us?" If just one God created us, and the Father, Son, and Holy Spirit each were involved in creation, then how are these three separate and different Gods? So, "LORD God" in Genesis 2:4 should be understood not as there being two Gods but one.

(2). Exodus 5:3: "Sacrifice to the LORD our God lest He fall on us with pestilence or the sword." But observe that the verse refers the LORD God as "He" not "Them." The pronoun evidences that only one Being is the referent.

(3). Leviticus 26:13: "I am the LORD your God who brought you out of the land of Egypt." But aside from the singularity of the pronoun "I," it can be noted that texts as Exodus 4:5 demonstrate that Moses taught that only one God was responsible for liberating the Hebrews and He is the LORD God."

(4). Numbers 23:19, 21: "God is not a man (and) The LORD his God is with him." The context shows that only one Individual is meant by the LORD God as He is not said not to be "men" but not to be a "man." (verse 19).

(5). Deuteronomy 10:12, 13: "Fear the LORD your God, to walk in all His ways...and to keep the commandments of the LORD." In addition to the LORD GOD again being identified by the singular "His," we should observe that the commandments are those given by only one Being, one God, not several (Psalm 119:115) See also Mark 7:9 "the commandment of God." God in the Greek in this verse is the genitive singular *theou*. As only one God gave the commandments, "LORD" and "God" are the same Being.

(6). Joshua 22:34: "The LORD is God." The unity of the divine Being is here demonstrated by the fact that "LORD" (*Jehovah i.e., Yahweh*) is in the singular form. It does not say "LORDS." So, the LORD is one God. And, just as there is only one *Jehovah* (Deuteronomy 6:4) so there also is only one *Elohim*: "Besides Me there is no *Elohim*." (Isaiah 44:6).

(7). Judges 2:12: "They forsook the LORD God of their fathers." However, their fathers had only one real God. See, for example,

Genesis 12:1-4 and the calling of Abraham where four times the LORD is called "I;" He is not called "We"!

One could proceed through the entire Old Testament providing such evidences. Yes, I know that Mormons teach that it is God the Son only who is *Jehovah*, and so references to LORD God are to be limited to only one God in the Godhead not the two others. But I believe that I have shown here and in chapter two that this this teaching is in error.

4. Mormons may say 1 Corinthians 8:5 shows there are many Gods.

> For even if there are so- called gods, whether in heaven or on earth (as there are many gods and many lords) yet for us there is one God, the Father of whom are all things, and we for Him; and one Lord Jesus Christ, through whom are all things, and through whom we live. (1 Corinthians 8:5,6)

As said above, Mormons grasp at any possibilities to find in the Bible proofs that there are many gods. However, in verse 4 we read, "there is no other God but one." Therefore, the idols mentioned in verse 4 are not really Gods.

5. Mormons may say that Jesus referred to other gods, therefore there are more Gods than one.

> Jesus answered them, is it not written in your law, "I said you are gods. If He called then god to

whom the word of God came (and the Scripture cannot be broken). (John 10:34)

Of whom is our Lord speaking? His referent is in Psalm 82. These are human judges tasked with the function to defend the poor and do justice. They were called "gods" because they worked under divine authority. But instead look at how they act and consider their future. Mormons would have you believe that these individuals who lacked understanding, who walked in darkness, and who were subject to death are Gods! If you really believe that such conditions are true of Gods, then, yes, be a Mormon.

6. Mormons may say that the plural *Elohim* means Gods.

The Mormon Elder B.H. Roberts, said to have been "a brilliant thinker," contends that the plural noun *Elohim* translated in the King James Version as "God" in Genesis 1 and all through the Old Testament means "Gods."[4] While it is true that *Elohim* is a plural noun, that does not require it to be understood as indicating that two or more Beings are the subjects of the verbs in, for example, Genesis chapter one. First note that while the noun is plural in form the verbs are all singular denoting that the Being doing the action of the verb is one.

For example: 1:1: God created; 1:3: God said; 1:4: God saw; 1:5: God called; 1:7: God made.

Second, competent Jewish scholars translated *Elohim* with the singular form of *Theos* (not the plural *Theoi*) when translating the Old Testament into Greek a couple of centuries before

Christ. Third, Jews understand *Elohim* as being one God as, for example, as taught in the midrash of 300-500 C.E called Bereshit Rabbah. But even more significant is that when the inspired author of Hebrews quoted from Psalm 45:6, "Your throne O *Elohim* is forever," he translated "*Elohim*" by the Greek singular "*Theos*." (Hebrews 1:8) So, Mormons are in contradiction to the inspired author of Hebrews! But how many Mormons realize this? The plural *Elohim* is used of God to indicate His greatness.

7. Mormons may say that Three divine Beings are alluded to in Acts 7:55, 56

> But he being full of the Holy Spirit, gazed into heaven and saw the glory of God, and Jesus standing at the right hand of God. (Acts 7:55)

The reader is invited to review the comment on Matthew 3:16, 17 above. "Jesus standing" cannot be a refence to the deity of Christ as in that divine nature Jesus fills the universe (Ephesians 4:24) and the universe was created through Him (Hebrews 1:2). Shall we believe that a man standing on two legs created all things? Well, if one is Mormon, I suppose so. But I prefer to believe that He who is standing is the one who was not before human but was made "like His brethren" (Hebrews 2:17) and "became flesh" (John 1:14) which He previously was not. As to being at the "right hand of God," that expression denotes being in a position of power as texts like Psalm 80:17 and 110:1 demonstrate.

8. Mormons may say that as Christ is the Son of the Father, He cannot be the same in nature as the Father.

Within evangelicalism there have been several understandings expressed regarding the meaning of "Son of God." One is that the Son in His deity eternally is "generated" by the Father" in an ongoing, undefined, process (see chapter 2). A second is that being "Son of" requires Christ who in His divinity is equal in essence with the Father nevertheless is eternally role subordinate to the Father. Yet another is that "son of" denotes being of the same kind. So, in the Old Testament "son of" can indicate membership in a profession or guild. A "son of the troop" would be a member of the troop. Then, "Son of God" would mean He is God. And, we can note that when Jesus said that He was "Son of God," the Jews accused Him of making Himself "equal with God" (not with Gods-John 5:18). So, given John 5:18 and Philippians 2:6 as well, in my opinion, "Son of God" means being God.

The reader is invited to read below to be reminded of how the same attributes existing between the Father and the Son evidence that these Two are equal. But not only are they equal in nature, They comprise only one Being as there is only one God:

"Besides Me there is no God" (Isaiah 44:6).

"I am God and there is no other" (Isaiah 46:9).

"The only God" (John 5:44).

"No other God but one" (1 Corinthians 8:4)

But, Christ is included that one God:

"The Word was God" (John 1:3)

"My Lord and my God" (John 20:28)

"Therefore God" (Hebrews 1:9)

"Our great God and Savior Jesus Christ" (Titus 2:13).

Some (see the New World Translation rendition of Titus 2:13) have supposed that while Christ is Savior, He is not identified as "God" in Titus 2:13. I hope the reader will forgive me for being a bit technical in regard to this text. It should be noted that in the original language of the New Testament when two singular nouns of the same case (God, Savior which here are both genitive singular) are joined by the conjunction (*kai*) and only the first noun is modified by the article ("the") then both nouns refer to the same individual. Christ, therefore, is both our Savior and our God. All praise to Him! (Note that Titus 2:13 does not say that He is "one of the Gods.")

9. Mormons may say that as the Bible repeatedly states that the LORD is "the God of gods" there must be many who are Gods.

> For the Lord your God is God of gods and Lord of lords. (Deuteronomy 10:17; Joshua 22:22; Daniel 11:36)

But these other "gods" were not gods at all but were "the work of men's hands-wood and stone." (2 Kings 19:18; Isaiah 37:19). They were but "molded gods." (Leviticus 19:4). Can we forget that Israel soon after being redeemed from Egypt made itself a golden calf which they then pronounced to be god and began worshipping as god? (Exodus 32) Likewise, that the Lord God is "God of gods" does not prove a plurality of divine beings but alludes instead to the false religions of those who make and worship idols. And, for Mormons to build their doctrine of deity on such texts which allude to these practices shows the extent of the Mormon willingness to depart from the biblical doctrine of God.

10. Mormons may say that as Christ was exalted by the Father in Philippians 2 and Psalm 45, Christ cannot be the same in being with the Father.

Were Mormons to simply acknowledge that when Christ became flesh He could not change in His deity (Hebrews 1:12; 2:9, 14, 17), then they would find that much in the Gospels would make more sense. Do Mormons really believe that God's nature falls asleep in a boat Mark 4:38) or does not know somethings (Mark 13:32) or sweats (Luke 22:44) or dies (John 19:33)? Yes, I guess they must. But were they to without qualification acknowledge that God is "almighty" (Genesis 17:1), I think they would question that Christ, as God, needs to take naps or is ignorant of some things or sweats fearing death or was murdered. To me it clearly is the case that such experiences as those are true only of His humanity not of His deity. But in Mormonism the difference between humanity and deity seems negligible. But in the Bible, that difference is extremely great.

So, in regard to the exaltation of Christ by the Father, we should feel obliged to inquire whether it is Christ as man or Christ as God who is exalted. For this purpose we can turn to Philippians 2:8,9 and read,

> And being found in the appearance of a man,
> He humbled Himself and became obedient to
> the point of death, even the death of the cross.
> Therefore God also has highly exalted Him.

It was as man, then, that Christ was exalted. The anointing of the Son in Psalm 45:7 clearly does not correspond to the exaltation of Christ in Philippians 2 since in the former the Son in majesty sits on an eternal throne. Nor is there anything in Psalm 45 to suggest that Christ was exalted into deity. But, in the latter the Son in humbleness dies on a cross. It therefore, follows that as Christ was exalted in His manhood, not in His deity, the exaltation of Christ does not prove Him to be a different Being than God the Father.

Before concluding this book, I would like to argue that as the Three Persons in God have the same attributes, the same titles, and do the same works that the Three are one God. The Father, of course, has not in New Testament interpretation often had His deity questioned. We should remind ourselves then of how the Son and the Spirit are equal to the Father in powers, titles, and works.

So, let's observe that the Son is said to be immutable (Hebrews 13:8), eternal (John 1:1), all powerful (Revelation 1:8), omnipresent (Ephesians 1:23) and omniscient (John 16:30). Also, note that the Son is given the same titles given the Father as God (John 20:28) and Lord. (Revelation 17:14). Furthermore, The Son was involved with the Father in both creation (Colossians 1:16) and salvation (1 Thessalonians 5:9). And, finally we should be reminded that His name is put on equal footing with that of the Father (Matthew 20:19). So, all of these things are said of Christ. But note: There is none like God except God Himself (Isaiah 46:9). So, Christ is included in that one God.

Likewise, the Holy Spirit is said in Scripture to be omnipresent (Psalm 139:7), omniscient (1 Corinthians 2:10) and eternal (Hebrews 9:4). Also, the Spirit is referred to as both Lord (2 Corinthians 3:17) and God (Acts 5:3, 4). And, the Spirit also is involved in both creation (Genesis 1:2) and salvation (John 3:8). Finally, we must recall that the Holy Spirit is put on the same footing as the Father (2 Corinthians 13:14). But, again note that there are none like God but God Himself! (Isaiah 46:9) So, the Holy Spirit is included in that one God.

Review questions chapter 4

1. What Mormon teaching does Deuteronomy 6:43 refute?

2. How does God creating indicate He is a Trinity?

3. Explain what shows Robertson's understanding of *Elohim* is incorrect.

4. How do Ephesians 4:24 and Colossians 3:10 define God's image in man?

5. Explain how John 4:6 and Colossians 1:17 can be harmonized.

6. Comment on the meaning of Philippians 2:6, 7.

7. What are some qualities of the true God?

8. How does Malachi 2:7 refute Mormon doctrine?

9. What shows that John 10:34 cannot refer to real Gods?

10. What evidences that Christ in His divinity was not baptized?

Endnotes chapter 4

1. Bruce R. McConkie. *Mormon Doctrine.* (Salt Lake, 1966), 257.

2. Daniel B. Wallace. *Greek Grammar Beyond the Basics.* (Grand Rapids: Zondervan, 1996), 378.

3. Brigham Young. *Discourses.* 7.333.

4. B.H. Roberts. *Mormon Doctrine of Deity,* (Bountiful Utah: Horizon, 1982), 139.

CPSIA information can be obtained
at www.ICGtesting.com
Printed in the USA
LVHW021628260921
698761LV00001B/115

9 781633 574083